Dylan Thomas: Selected Poems

Dylan Thomas

Selected Poems

EDITED WITH AN INTRODUCTION
AND NOTES BY

WALFORD DAVIES

LONDON AND TORONTO

J. M. DENT & SONS LTD

Copyright © 1934, 1937, 1938, 1939, 1941, 1944, 1945,
1955, 1956, 1962, 1965, 1966, 1967, 1971,
by the Trustees for the Copyrights of Dylan Thomas

Introduction and Notes © Walford Davies 1974

All rights reserved
No part of this publication may be reproduced, stored
in a retrieval system, or transmitted in any form
or by any means, electronic, mechanical, photocopying,
recording or otherwise, without the prior permission of
J. M. Dent & Sons Ltd.

Printed in Great Britain by
Biddles Ltd, Guildford, Surrey
for
J. M. DENT & SONS LTD
Aldine House, Albemarle Street, London

First published 1974
Reprinted 1975, 1977

ISBN 0 460 09618 4

ACKNOWLEDGMENTS

Grateful acknowledgment is made to the Trustees of the Hardy Estate,
The Macmillan Company of Canada and Macmillan London and
Basingstoke for their permission to use lines from 'To an Unborn Pauper
Child' by Thomas Hardy from *Collected Poems*; to William Empson and
Chatto & Windus Ltd for lines from 'Camping Out' by William Empson
from *Collected Poems*; and to the Oxford University Press for lines from
'Stormy Day' by W. R. Rodgers from *Collected Poems*.

CONTENTS

[v]

For Jason and Damian

INTRODUCTION

I

> But, to start with, if one view makes a bit of poetry very
> good, and another makes it very bad, the author's
> intention is inherently likely to be the one that makes it
> good; especially if we know that he writes well some-
> times.   (William Empson, in *Milton's God*)

The most obvious feature of Dylan Thomas's reputation as a poet
has been the stunning disagreement critics have shown on the
subject of his achievement. The debate (though gang-warfare
might be a more accurate term) has been peculiar in the range of
emotions it has aroused, and it must be conceded at the start that
empty claims and lunatic explanations have been as prominent on
the favourable side as silly insults and stubborn prejudice have
been on the other. The pity is that voices either side of the argu-
ment have been most memorable when they have been most shrill.
Edith Sitwell's kind but always nebulous advertisements of
Thomas's power early on, or Philip Toynbee's tactless claim in
1952 that Thomas was the greatest living English poet, are
unfortunately better known even today than T. S. Eliot's quiet
remark 'I certainly regarded him always as a poet of considerable
importance'. Similarly, books which make ridiculous claims for
Thomas's erudition, prompting as they do insulting reactions to
what has come to be known as the 'Dylan Thomas industry', have
diluted the effect of more sober and impressive examinations in
books by R. N. Maud or T. H. Jones, or in essays by William
Empson, John Bayley, or John Wain.

From the start there has been felt the understandable need to
correct over-fulsome praise. But that a considerable amount of

over-compensating has been done seems clear. Thomas's most strident opponents seem often to have ignored a fact as basic to criticism as it is to law: that one will not get even a conviction for theft on a charge of murder. In his Clark Lectures at Cambridge, printed as *The Crowning Privilege* in 1955, Robert Graves did not claim that Thomas's poem 'If my head hurt a hair's foot' was difficult or that it demanded patience; he simply said that it made no sense at all. (Indeed he bet a pound note on the fact, but refused to pay when M. J. C. Hodgart produced a perfectly clear account of the poem.) Or take the case of the *Scrutiny* critics. They seem to have assumed that the principles implied in their excellent treatment of classic poets spoke volumes in the gaps of what was a very scrappy and insulting treatment of Thomas, as indeed of contemporary poetry as a whole. Where Thomas was concerned, the Scrutineers spared only a glance. Their treatment of Thomas was a victory of tone rather than of demonstration, and that tone has a stentorian ring even in the final Index to the series, where Thomas figures under headings like 'failure to mature'; 'repudiated by critics with high standards'; or 'mythology dismissed'. The two most formidable critics to have stood out against Thomas are probably Donald Davie and George Steiner.[1] But surely we can expect that, when they level the respective accusations of 'pseudo syntax' and 'imposter', they should do so in something more than a passing reference, and share more than one quotation between them. In contrast, David Holbrook looked long and hard, but only to find that Dylan Thomas was psychologically damaged at source.[2] Holbrook, very much concerned with the kind of *person* he thinks Thomas to have been, fails to make the necessary division between (as T. S. Eliot once put it) the man who suffers and the mind which creates, or (as W. B. Yeats put it) between the poet who writes the poem and 'the bundle of accident and incoherence that sits down to breakfast'.

[1] See Donald Davie, *Articulate Energy* (Routledge and Kegan Paul 1955); and George Steiner, *Language and Silence* (Faber 1967).
[2] See David Holbrook, *Llareggub Revisited* (Bodley Head 1962) and *Dylan Thomas: The Code of Night* (The Athlone Press, 1972).

Some such overkill is apparent in many areas of the anti-Thomas faction. Let us take a representative example in the form of Geoffrey Grigson, a critic of real discrimination both as Editor of *New Verse*, an important poetry magazine of the 1930s, and more generally. Early on, Grigson was a friend of Thomas's both in the personal sense and in that he published nine of Thomas's poems, plus some reviews and other contributions by the poet, in *New Verse* between 1934 and 1937. In his book *The Harp of Aeolus* (1948), however, Grigson published a bitter attack on Thomas's poetry. In its general principles, the essay validly re-affirms Hopkins's warnings about 'frigidities' and 'untruths to nature' in poetic imagery. But what is disconcerting, indeed insulting, is the *way* in which Grigson applies his principles to the case of Dylan Thomas. One could demonstrate what seems to be Grigson's sheer prejudice against Thomas's use of half-rhymes, his rhythms, or his central concern with the human body. But I shall content myself with the following example.

In the middle of Grigson's essay, we find this:

No more, no less construable is:

> There was a saviour –
> In the churches of his tears
> There was calm to be done in his safe unrest
> Children kept from the sun
> On to the ground when a man has died
> To hear the golden note turn in a groove,
> Silence, silence to do, when earth grew loud
> In the jails and studies of his keyless smiles.

—a stanza upon which Mr Thomas's explorers and admirers should meditate, for reasons which I shall give later.

Over the page, Grigson returns to cock a snook at anyone who had in the meantime been admiring the quoted lines. The stanza, you see, is bogus. Grigson simply put eight completely unrelated lines from 'There was a Saviour' next to each other and claimed triumphantly to have sprung a trap—because, as he says over the page, 'it reads, I am convinced, as authentically as most of Mr Thomas's stanzas'. One wonders what sort of helpless audience Grigson had in mind whom he could expect either to fall into the trap and blush from embarrassment, or wink in approval at such a ploy. But quite apart from the cheapness of the trick, and quite apart also from the fact that Grigson misquotes his fifth line, let us consider the claim which the deceit was designed to serve.

The obvious thing to do is to quote a genuine stanza from Thomas's poem, to stand against Mr Grigson's cynical mock-up:

> There was a saviour
> Rarer than radium,
> Commoner than water, crueller than truth;
> Children kept from the sun
> Assembled at his tongue
> To hear the golden note turn in a groove,
> Prisoners of wishes locked their eyes
> In the jails and studies of his keyless smiles.

A fundamental difference is immediately obvious. The authentic stanza has a rhythmic convincingness. By that, I do not mean just the music of certain phrases or lines, but the rhythmic backbone which makes Thomas's stanza a pliant unit. The Grigson forgery is rhythmically inert. If it was an accusation of inertness that he wished to make, he would have done more honestly to try and argue from fact than fiction—indeed, to try and *argue* in the first place. And if a related accusation was meant to be one against emptiness of meaning, all one can say is that fact once again ruins his fiction. For while Grigson's jumbled lines add up to nothing (despite his amazing claim that they are 'just-construable'!), Thomas's actual stanza gets down to real work. It establishes a point of departure by evoking the historical Christ, and initiates his argument that Christ's message has been corrupted by Christians into selfish wish-fulfilment and arid debate. What is more: by quoting the lines as Thomas actually wrote them, we see how the

[4]

poet makes his form into an extra comment on his meaning because for this confrontation with 'Christianity', Thomas has ironically used the stanza-form of Milton's 'On the Morning of Christ's Nativity'. Did Mr Grigson recognize the fact, and choose to ignore it; or did he just not recognize it? 'There was a Saviour' may not be one of Thomas's finest achievements, but it is more certainly not the lifeless sham that Grigson's piece of glum sabotage would have us believe.

We need no longer fall prey to this kind of bullying. I have used the example of Geoffrey Grigson because he conveniently focuses the kind of hostility which grew up slowly with Thomas's also increasing popularity, as it was widened beyond a narrowly academic taste by his gradual emergence as the writer of excellent comic prose, and as broadcaster, script-writer and lecturer. A new reader need not be afraid to look such hostility straight in the face. Indeed, some impression of Thomas's stature seems implicit in the very insistence of that reaction against him: his reputation may be disparaged, but it cannot be ignored. Writing in outright praise of Dylan Thomas in a recent number of *The Spectator*, Gabriel Pearson struck what seems to me to be the right kind of note: 'The legend is still an un-negotiated legacy, fraught with predictable discomfort however you play it, whether with aloofness or bold enthusiasm. Either way, Thomas remains powerful, disreputable and not to be patronized.'

Association of Thomas's poetry with Surrealism or with the 'New Romantic' and 'New Apocalypse' poets probably accounted for much of the opposition in the 'thirties and 'forties. As far as Surrealism is concerned, it is important to stress that few poets deserve less the charge of 'automatic writing' than Thomas. He himself felt genuinely insulted when Richard Church hinted such a charge in a letter of 1935, and he had no time at all for the work of David Gascoyne, the leading English Surrealist poet of the 'thirties. Thomas, a provincial young man fascinated by the weird fashions of London artistic society in that decade, certainly turned up at the 'International Surrealist Exhibition' of 1936 and joined in the fun by passing around cups of boiled string, asking 'Weak

[5]

or strong?' And deeper than the level of fun, it is clear that Surrealism tinged the imagination of many poets who could not be simply labelled 'Surrealist'. Springing out of Dadaism in wartime France, Surrealism had already had some influence on the imagery of early Eliot. In this sense, Thomas was very much of his own time. But when he writes, in 'On a Wedding Anniversary',

> From every true or crater
> Carrying cloud, Death strikes their house

is Grigson right in claiming that 'Clouds with craters are like veins with ears', that the words 'are nearly automatic'? Given that the poem is obviously about death in one of the Second World War air-raids, what is wrong with the image's obvious meaning: that the cloud-like formation of dropping bombs will produce a crater where they land? But the charge of 'automatic writing' is refuted also by more concrete evidence: that of Thomas's manuscript work-sheets and of his correspondence with Vernon Watkins from 1936 onwards. These show us a painfully conscious craftsman at work. Thomas was justified in claiming that his poetry did not 'flow', but was rather 'hewn', as out of stone.

As for the 'New Romantic' poets like George Barker, W. S. Graham, and W. R. Rodgers, or the 'New Apocalypse' poets led by Henry Treece and J. F. Hendry: these came into gradual prominence in the 'thirties and 'forties, and clearly recognized in Thomas a meaningful alternative to the more intellectual and politically committed talents of the poets grouped by reputation around W. H. Auden. But Thomas cannot be held responsible for their mediocrity; he saw himself as no part, let alone a leader, of any 'movement' whatsoever. Grigson was in fact associating Thomas with the 'New Romanticism' of the 'forties (the title of his essay—'How Much Me Now Your Acrobatics Amaze'—was a line from a poem by George Barker). Critics have a duty to differentiate between talents, and not blur the issue by implying sameness where closer attention would show it to be bogus. And yet, paradoxically, Grigson perhaps did less disservice to Thomas

[6]

than is done nowadays by those who condescendingly claim that Thomas was simply 'the best of that group'. That is exactly the force of Gabriel Pearson's warning, which I quoted above, that Thomas is not to be patronized.

To some degree, the 1940s were Thomas's decade. In the 1930s there had been felt, for one thing, the dwarfing presence of the century's two greatest poets, Yeats and Eliot. Yeats was then drawing to the end of his magnificent career, but his *New Poems* (1938) and his posthumous *Last Poems* (1939) stood strongly at the end of that decade. Eliot, whose *Collected Poems* appeared in 1936, was very much the on-going genius, with the *Four Quartets* as such still to be written when the decade closed. But since a generation tends to identify with its younger contemporaries, the real signature stamped on the 'thirties had been that of Auden. In the 'forties, however, with Yeats dead, with the *Four Quartets* bringing Eliot's poetry to an obvious fulness in 1944, and with Auden in America, hindsight probably allowed some to feel that the 'thirties had in reality been shared by Auden and Thomas together. Certainly, as the 'forties wore on, Thomas came more and more into his own. The publication of his fourth volume, *Deaths and Entrances*, in 1946, including as it did more immediately approachable poems like 'Poem in October', 'A Refusal to Mourn', 'The Hunchback in the Park', and 'Fern Hill', and his increasing popularity as a broadcaster, gave Thomas a very real, and certainly an unignorable position. And of course the pattern of his fame continued into the 'fifties, until his tragically early death on a lecture-tour in America in 1953. In 1952, his *Collected Poems* set his achievement in front of all interested parties, friends and enemies alike. At one moment he had looked like a natural survivor; in another, he had gone and done the one unforgivable thing—gone out with a bang. This sense of climax, and the large-scale sense of shock which greeted his death, focused uncompromisingly the degree and nature of his celebrity.

Particularly noticeable in the 1940s was the way in which Thomas's reputation as a poet had come to be identified with his legend as a man. To many, of course, a poet who looked and acted like one was welcome. And to some degree this enabled him to reach a wider audience than serious poetry normally does. But for those who decried his qualities as a poet, it is clear that his drinking habits and his colossal carelessness as to his personal welfare must have seemed to be extensions of a freewheeling lack of discipline also affecting his verse. For our present purposes, however, the most useful manifestation of such a view is a retrospective one. I refer to the particular reaction which was felt in the preoccupations and techniques of the new generation of poets who emerged in the 1950s. Any young reader approaching Dylan Thomas's poetry at the present time does so in a literary atmosphere initiated and still controlled by that generation.

The poets involved—Kingsley Amis, Donald Davie, Philip Larkin, John Wain, D. J. Enright, for example—were given some kind of unified weight, despite their differences, by their collection into an anthology called *New Lines*, edited by Robert Conquest in 1956. (Another *New Lines* anthology came out in 1963.) As early as 1954, the group had been hallowed by a journalistic title—'The Movement'. By no means did all the poets involved think Thomas negligible. But the very assumptions of their work—control of emotion, understatement, sober diction—show clear signs of a reversal of Thomas's emotional expansiveness, his rhetoric, and verbal inventiveness. In short, they sought to re-intellectualize the world of poetry, and superannuate the 'Romantic' or 'Bardic' concept of the poet. There can be no doubt that English poetry of the present time has gained from the decisiveness of their efforts. But it should also be a self-evident truth that Dylan Thomas's quality, like that of Hopkins, does not itself depend on his being good copy for later poets with radically different gifts, and a different order of experience to explore.

My point is that, where reaction to Thomas is tied in with new creative needs, that reaction is already beyond the area of in-fighting, of rights and wrongs, or the need for vengeful value-judgments. In contrast, those detractors who were also Thomas's actual contemporaries, like Geoffrey Grigson, often sound as if it was merely too early to have another successful poet who relied so

[8]

little on what Eliot or Auden could teach him. In a 'Postscript 1966' to his brilliant critical book *Purity of Diction in English Verse*, which first appeared in 1952, Donald Davie shows how this treatment of diction in Eighteenth and Nineteenth Century poetry might well have acted as a manifesto for the 'Movement' poets, and significantly adds that much in the book was 'a reaction from the tawdry amoralism of a London Bohemia which had destroyed Dylan Thomas, the greatest talent of the generation before ours'. It is Davie's necessary independence as a poet which saves that description from being simple condescension. Clearing the air of smoke is very different from shouting from your corner of the field that your bonfire isn't burning as brightly as Dylan Thomas's.

But the new reader of Dylan Thomas, approaching his work perhaps for the first time in this selection, doesn't even run the danger of condescension in the first place. He has that refreshing freedom which comes with a real sense of distance. Adding some measure of objectivity is the fact that the last two decades have in any case seen reactions also to the 'Movement' poets, reactions to a reaction. Reading the revised edition of A. Alvarez's anthology, *The New Poetry* (Penguin 1966), is a good way of seeing how quickly the sobering aims of the 'Movement' came to be accused of low-key 'gentility', the word Alvarez uses in his Introduction to limit the achievement of Philip Larkin. Alvarez places considerable emphasis on the work of Sylvia Plath and Ted Hughes, both of whom often make us think of Dylan Thomas. Thus it is not surprising to find Alvarez, again in his Introduction, saying that 'Thomas was not only a fine rhetorician, he also, in his early poems, had something rather original to say'. As it happens, I think Alvarez's view of Larkin does a gross injustice to an outstanding poet. But what is to be welcomed is this sign of objectivity where Dylan Thomas is concerned, and this emphasis on *meaning*. The influential success of Alvarez's *The New Poetry* suggests that some measure of balance has been restored. Whatever disagreements lie in store as to the fortunes of the younger generation of poets, there are signs that Thomas's reputation will be less and less damaged by the heat. The new reader is already in a position to

[9]

refuse to make an exclusive choice between two important poets as utterly different as Philip Larkin and Dylan Thomas. If I may borrow some lines of Larkin's out of context:

> I don't say, one bodies the other
> One's spiritual truth;
> But I do say it's hard to lose either,
> When you have both.

II

What I propose to do now is select one of Dylan Thomas's early poems and give some account of it, in the hope that this will be some guide as to how he can be approached. On the whole, new readers will probably find the later poems easier of access. I select an early poem because it was at this period (say from 1930 to 1934, when Thomas was between 16 and 20 years of age) that he was first discovering an independent voice in poetry. By grounding my discussion in one poem, I am inviting the reader to test my comments against his own reading. I shall, however, move away from my chosen example as the need arises. My aim is to characterize some main features of Thomas's early style and preoccupations.

The poem I have chosen is 'I see the boys of summer', written in April 1934. If we had been part of the poetry-reading public in that year, this would have been the first poem we would have encountered on opening Dylan Thomas's *18 Poems*. Thomas himself thought it representative enough to stand at the entrance of his first collection. In the present edition, it will be found on page 40. The first thing the reader should do, then, is read 'I see the boys of summer' two or three times.

The first thing to strike us is the absence of a conventional title. It is characteristic of especially an early poem to make its opening words serve this purpose. First-line titles of this kind suggest a refusal to abstract 'meaning' prematurely, or a refusal to forecast a narrative other than the one we can possess only *in the reading*.

[10]

Instead of directing our attention to a graspable whole as more conventional titles do—and titles, we remember, are the first words we read of any poem—Thomas's early titles merely warn us that we will have to start again at the beginning of each poem's narrative. This is not a case of Thomas being anti-social. Indeed, such titles carry an attractive invitation to listen-in to a poem's narrative event, as can be suggested if we quote some characteristic examples in isolation: 'Light breaks where no sun shines', 'Especially when the October wind', 'The force that through the green fuse drives the flower'.

Having read the poem itself, the reader will have felt that certain concepts (e.g. fruitfulness and aridity) have been communicated before he can clearly describe what the poem, in the usual sense, is 'about'. He will also have noticed how such concepts are constantly being set in opposition to each other. In the first line, for example, 'the boys of *summer*' are 'in their *ruin*'. The reader is, in fact, already in touch with the poem's main theme, for that theme is certainly concerned with the forces of growth and decay as they underlie our general sense of life. But in my words the theme is merely an abstract idea; Thomas's actual poem is concrete, its language almost tangible.

We are also aware that the poem gives us the sense, not only of a general theme, but of an actual situation. After all, the speaker is drawing our attention to '*these* boys of light', and in the final section even addresses them as '*you* boys of summer'. We feel, in other words, that the 'boys of summer' of the first two stanzas are in a real sense boys, however private may be Thomas's feelings about them. In the same way, the 'summer children in their mothers' of the third and fourth stanzas are actual unborn children in the womb. (In a letter of the same month as the poem, Thomas wrote: 'I see the unborn children struggling up the hill in their mothers, beating on the jailing slab of the womb, little realizing what a smugger prison they wish to leap into.') By the end of the first section of the poem, the speaker has made a specific accusation: that the boys he sees around him are turning that which is fruitful and life-giving into that which is sour or frozen;

[11]

and that those children still to be born will grow up to do the same. What Thomas is drawing attention to seems to be a code of conduct which causes this denial of natural impulse. We feel that the implied subject of the poem is the nature of a certain kind of society which places restraints on natural sexuality. It seems reasonable to suspect that the immediate Welsh Nonconformist, puritanical society in which he was growing up is in Thomas's mind, a society which encourages 'frigid threads of doubt and dark' (stanza two). In such a society, youth is, and always will be, old before its time. Though this reaction to his immediate social context is not given the same measure of emphasis in all the early poems, the new reader would do well to bear in mind, while reading them, the idea of a young adolescent trying to approach the facts of life, death and sexuality without using the moral language in which society usually teaches us to think.

Hints as to how the rest of 'I see the boys of summer' develops will be found in the Notes. Our present aim is to try and decide what *kind* of poem it is. In theme it reminds us of Blake, especially the *Songs of Experience*, and possibly of D. H. Lawrence, both of whom influenced the young Dylan Thomas. Blake comes specifically to mind because of his conviction that society enchains the natural impulses of childhood and replaces physical instinct with abstract morality. And the comparison holds good because, like Thomas, Blake developed a highly personal range of images and symbols with which to body forth that vision. (The reader might look at poems like Blake's 'The Sick Rose', 'The Garden of Love', 'London', 'Infant Sorrow'.) But in order to draw out the stylistic characteristics of 'I see the boys of summer', I shall introduce a very different kind of poem, by Thomas Hardy. Its title is 'To an Unborn Pauper Child', and its first four stanzas will give an adequate impression of the kind of poem it is:

> Breathe not, hid Heart: cease silently,
> And though thy birth-hour beckons thee,
>   Sleep the long sleep:
>   The Doomsters heap

Travails and teens around us here,
And Time-wraiths turn our songsingings to fear.

Hark, how the peoples surge and sigh,
And laughters fail, and greetings die:
    Hopes dwindle; yea,
    Faiths waste away,
Affections and enthusiasms numb;
Thou canst not mend these things if thou dost come.

Had I the ear of wombèd souls
Ere their terrestrial chart unrolls,
    And thou wert free
    To cease, or be,
Then would I tell thee all I know,
And put it to thee: Wilt thou take Life so?

Vain vow! No hint of mine may hence
To theeward fly: to thy locked sense
    Explain none can
    Life's pending plan:
Thou wilt thy ignorant entry make
Though skies spout fire and blood and nations quake.

The comparison is a convenient one because Hardy, too, is concerned with the kind of society the child will be born into, and concerned with the difference between potential and reality. (In a different way, the reader might also like to compare Hardy's poem with Thomas's 'If my head hurt a hair's foot'.) But more striking are the obvious differences between Hardy's and Thomas's use of language. It will be seen that Hardy's language is more discursive—one might say more 'public'. It carries Hardy's ideas more openly, more obviously. Indeed, we are more aware of the ideas than of the words which carry them. One reason for this is Hardy's sequence of abstract words—'travails', 'teens', 'fear', 'laughters', 'greetings', 'hopes', 'faiths', and so on. It is also clear that Society as

[13]

such is in the *foreground* of Hardy's poem, and is being obviously 'talked *about*'. As a result, the poem has a directly moral, humane tone. I suppose what I am basically claiming is that we would not feel it impossibly difficult to give some account of the poem in paraphrase.

'I see the boys of summer', on the other hand, seems from the very first line to be beyond any paraphrase which wouldn't seem a gross simplification of its effects. The first thing to stress, as I have already suggested, is the concreteness of its language, though a better word would be 'literalness'. Images like 'gold tithings', 'soils', 'winter floods', 'cargoed apples' in the first stanza are not in the ordinary sense metaphors or symbols. That is to say, they do not 'stand for' other things. This could be demonstrated by the sheer impossibility of finding point-for-point equivalents for them. Rather, what Thomas is doing is creating what we might call a network of images which replaces the real world, while still expecting us to know what 'soils', 'floods', and 'apples' are. Thomas always insisted that his early poems should be read 'literally', and this is exactly what he meant. We remember that when T. S. Eliot was once asked to explain the meaning of his line 'Lady, three white leopards sat under a juniper-tree', he replied, 'It means Lady, three white leopards sat under a juniper tree'. What both Eliot and Thomas were insisting on was the fact that poetry of this kind is irreducible, that it cannot, like a suitcase, be unpacked of its meanings. Which is, of course, not the same thing as saying that it doesn't have any meaning. We can still talk of the ideas of such a poem (indeed, we have already been doing so in Thomas's case): but the ideas are ideas brought to birth in our minds while reading. They are not presented *as* ideas in the poem.

Two shaping developments in the history of early Twentieth-Century poetry were Imagism, which insisted on the hard ordinary literalness of individual images; and Symbolism, which had its origins in Nineteenth-Century French poetry, and held that a poem need not obviously relate to realities outside itself, that it was its own verbal world. Thomas's early Notebook poetry often illustrates similar assumptions, but his first successful poems were neither Imagist nor Symbolist in the full sense. He would naturally have deplored the emotional poverty and formal thinness of the Imagists proper; and, as for strict Symbolist poetry, it is quite clear that in Thomas's early poems the realities of birth, sex, and death are *there*. In a school magazine essay on 'Modern Poetry' in 1929, when he was 16, he had shown himself to be precociously aware of the various ingredients that had contributed to the making of poetic Modernism in poetry. The experimentalism of Eliot's generation was already literary history by the time Thomas was writing his first mature poems in the early 1930s, but the way in which that generation had freed poetry from ordinary discourse (the need to 'talk *about*' things in poems) was still a potent legacy. With these considerations in mind, Thomas could have said, with Yeats, 'I have no speech but symbol, the pagan speech I made/ Amid the dreams of youth.'

It seems important to remember, then, that Thomas's generation could reap the benefits of those factors which had, two decades earlier, gone into the making of modern poetry. The revival of interest in the Metaphysical poets of the Seventeenth-Century, for example. 'I see the boys of summer' may not furnish the best examples of what Thomas clearly owes to Donne, but it does illustrate the Metaphysical method of foreshortening the distance between Life and Death, of constantly seeing one in terms of the other. And the poem's last line—'O see the poles are kissing as they cross'—seems clearly related to the Metaphysical kind of image.

Another influence on modern poetry is one which happened as if by accident. The poems of the Victorian Gerard Manley Hopkins were first fully published only in 1918. Eliot's generation was by then already in full swing, so that it was natural for Hopkins to influence the younger poets growing up in the 1920s, whose real decade was to be the 'thirties. Once again, 'I see the boys of summer' may not seem particularly Hopkinsian in its use of language. But I shall argue that Hopkins is in fact a real consideration here. In his later poems, Thomas makes more obvious use of Hopkins, even down to the use of a phrase like 'high there' (from Hopkins's 'The Windhover') in 'In country sleep'. But to get back to the 1930s, we need to differentiate between two different ways in which Hopkins influenced the poets of Thomas's generation. One way involved obvious and unashamed imitation. Early Auden, with his delight in trying out other poets' voices and techniques, could write good Hopkinsian pastiche, and know it. Lesser poets seemed less self-consciously to write as if they had themselves newly formed this verbal excitement. Here is the opening of W. R. Rodgers's poem 'Stormy Day':

> O look how the loops and balloons of bloom
> Bobbing on long strings from the finger-ends
> And knuckles of the lurching cherry-tree
> Heap and hug, elbow and part, this wild day,
> Like a careless carillon cavorting;
> And the beaded whips of the beeches splay
> And dip like anchored weeds round a drowned rock,
> And hovering effortlessly the rooks
> Hang on the wind's effrontery as if
> On hooks, then loose their hold and slide away
> Like sleet sidewards down the warm swimming sweep
> Of wind.

In contrast to this surface excitement, however, we have the case of poets who were more meaningfully, if less obviously, indebted to Hopkins's example. For instance, no one would immediately include William Empson in a list of those poets who most obviously reflected Hopkinsian virtues. 'Camping Out' is a good example of Empsonian poetry at its best. It opens:

> And now she cleans her teeth into the lake:
> Gives it (God's grace) for her own bounty's sake
> What morning's pale and the crisp mist debars:
> Its glass of the divine (that Will could break)
> Restores, beyond Nature: or lets Heaven take
> (Itself being dimmed) her pattern, who half awake
> Milks between rocks a straddled sky of stars.

[16   ]

Yet look at lines 2, 3 and 7 of this stanza. They illustrate the best feature of Hopkins's influence on modern poetry. That feature is not simple flashy excitement, but a feeling of genuine *weight* and *density* in the lines. A later line from Empson's poem—'Slowly madonna through-assumes the skies'—illustrates the same lesson.

An indication of the authenticity and individuality of Thomas's early poems is the fact that they, too, could do without Hopkins's most obvious effects. But the Hopkinsian qualities of what I have called weight and density (our feeling that lines have been sensuously relished and articulated in the mouth) are definitely there, and 'I see the boys of summer' illustrates the fact. For Hopkins and Thomas, language is not a cool set of signs *pointing* to the weight and density of things. For them, words are themselves 'things', with their own rhythmic, physical life. This is what I mean when I say that ideas are not 'carried' by such language; a Thomas image is not simply a thought translated. I suppose Ted Hughes is the poet who nowadays gives us a similar impression. But if we compare an image from Hughes's poem 'Thrushes',

> the shark's mouth
> That hungers down the blood-smell even to a leak of its own
> Side and devouring of itself

with one from Thomas's 'Poem on his birthday',

> The rippled seals streak down
> To kill and their own tide daubing blood
> Slides good in the sleek mouth

we recognize the difference between Hughes's intellectualization of the physical and Thomas's deeper empathy with it. The difference is still in the use of language.

Other thoughts prompted by 'I see the boys of summer' could, of course, detain us longer. It is clear, for example, how strenuous is Thomas's sense of form: the consistency of its stanzaic shape, or its strict syllabic count of 11, 7, 10, 8, 8, 10, broken in only one line. To some degree, this is the sign of a Welshman's regard for what we could call resistant form. Our sense of the poem as a 'made object' is strong. Or we might develop the impression it gives us of an adolescent sensibility trying to get to grips with the sexual quality of life, and the awareness of death. Or the strong impression of a young man exploring a personal vision, instead of the public 'political' commitment which was already the fashion by the time Thomas started to write his first good poems. A point certainly worth mentioning is the way in which 'I see the boys of summer' contrasts with the more open narratives and the more recognizable natural world of Thomas's later poems. (The shift from the earlier to the later mode is his subject in 'Once it was the colour of saying', which the reader could approach as a transitional poem.) But these, amongst others, are aspects which the present selection of poems will in any case bring to mind.

Though I have included one or two minor poems, I think the selection itself does represent the main characteristics of Thomas's achievement. Each reader will promote or limit that achievement according to his individual response to the poems which follow. Something I would myself wish to affirm is that as a poet Dylan Thomas has the great and simple virtue of memorability. And that much never can be obsolete.

III

A word finally about the Notes. In a review of Dylan Thomas's *Collected Poems*, William Empson mentioned his satisfaction at being told the source of the name 'Mnetha' in Thomas's 'Before I knocked'. He went on to say, 'I think an annotated edition of Dylan Thomas ought to be prepared as soon as possible, and that a detail like that ought to go in briefly, but it would be hard to decide what else ought to go in.' I quote Professor Empson to agree with that last comment. I think it important to stress that the Notes at the end of this volume do not seek to explain everything, and nothing is by any one of them explained away. It is taken for granted that no two readers would always agree on what constitutes a difficulty in the first place, let alone agree on what solves it.

The aims of my Notes have been four-fold: 1 *To state the date of each poem.* The poems are arranged chronologically, except for the 'Author's Prologue'. Where the dates are not dates of composition, they are those provided by either references in Thomas's letters or the fact of first publication. It would be over-fussy to add all the details but the reader can assume that each date is the first reliable date for the completion of the poem in its final form. 2 *To suggest where relevant another poem by Thomas or by a different poet, for the interest of comparison.* Such comparisons are a useful way in which to widen the discussion of a Thomas poem. I do not mean to suggest that any two poems thus juxtaposed are in theme and quality identical; and anyway, I am assuming that when I say 'Compare', the reader will also contrast. 3 *To offer a broad indication of the poem's theme.* The reader will of course be aware that no valuable poem can be reduced to a summary or paraphrase. W. Y. Tindall's words are a good reminder: 'Idea, replacing poem, will drive out marvel.' My general description of a poem's theme is designed to facilitate a new reader's first entry into the poem by giving something around which he can marshal his own responses and impressions, whether in agreement or disagreement with my own. 4 *To annotate certain local difficulties or points of interest.* Here I have not aimed at absolute uniformity in the points selected for comment, beyond of course choosing the details which seemed most obviously to present difficulty. Otherwise, I have sought to suggest the variety of surface characteristics one encounters in reading Dylan Thomas.

Useful companions to a study of these poems would be the poet's *Letters to Vernon Watkins* (Dent 1957), his *Selected Letters* (Dent 1966), and Constantine FitzGibbon's *The Life of Dylan Thomas* (Dent 1965). Of the many critical studies those by Derek Stanford (Dent 1954) and T. H. Jones (Oliver & Boyd 1963) would be a fair introduction for a new reader. But more im-

[19]

mediately helpful perhaps would be Thomas's own reading of many of those poems on record. Certainly, after close examination of any poem, one's outstanding duty is to put it back together again with the aid of the spoken voice, whether the poet's or the reader's own.

CHRONOLOGY OF MAIN DATES

22 Oct. 1914	Dylan Thomas born in Swansea.
Sept. 1925	Enters Swansea Grammar School, where his father was Senior English Master.
27 Apr. 1930	Starts the first of the 'Notebooks' into which he copied his poems (the Notebooks continued up until Apr. 1934).
Aug. 1931	Leaves school. Employed as Reporter on *South Wales Daily Post* until Nov. 1932.
Mar. 1933	First poem published in London (*And death shall have no dominion*).
Aug. 1933	First visit to London.
Sept. 1933	First poem published in 'Poet's Corner' of the *Sunday Referee*.
22 Apr. 1934	Wins Book Prize of 'Poet's Corner', i.e. the *Sunday Referee*'s sponsorship of his first collection of poems.
Mar. – Nov. 1934	Several visits to London.
10 Nov. 1934	Moves to live in London.
Dec. 1934	*18 Poems* published.
Apr. 1936	Meets Caitlin Macnamara.
10 Sept. 1936	*Twenty-Five Poems* published.
11 July 1937	Marries Caitlin Macnamara.
May 1938	First moved to live in Laugharne, Carmarthenshire.
Jan. 1939	First son (Llewelyn) born.
24 Aug. 1939	*The Map of Love* published (poems and stories).
4 Apr. 1940	*Portrait of the Artist as a Young Dog* published.
July 1940	Leaves Laugharne for London.
Sept. 1940	Begins work as script-writer for films.

1940–1942	Living partly in London, partly in Wales.
Late 1942	Brings wife and son to live in Chelsea.
Mar. 1943	First daughter (Aeronwy) born.
1943	Continuous work as broadcaster begins.
Summer 1944– summer 1945	Living at New Quay, Cardiganshire.
Summer 1945– spring 1946	Living in London.
7 Feb. 1946	*Deaths and Entrances* published.
Mar. 1946– May 1949	Living in or near Oxford.
Spring 1947	Visits Italy.
Mar. 1949	Visits Prague.
May 1949	Laugharne again becomes his main home (The Boat House).
July 1949	Second son (Colm) born.
Feb.–June 1950	First American tour.
Jan.–May 1952	Second American tour.
10 Nov. 1952	*Collected Poems* published.
15 Dec. 1952	The poet's father dies.
April–June 1953	Third American tour.
Oct. 1953	Leaves on final American tour.
9 Nov. 1953	Dies in New York City.

AUTHOR'S PROLOGUE

This day winding down now
At God speeded summer's end
In the torrent salmon sun,
In my seashaken house
On a breakneck of rocks   5
Tangled with chirrup and fruit,
Froth, flute, fin and quill
At a wood's dancing hoof,
By scummed, starfish sands
With their fishwife cross   10
Gulls, pipers, cockles, and sails,
Out there, crow black, men
Tackled with clouds, who kneel
To the sunset nets,
Geese nearly in heaven, boys   15
Stabbing, and herons, and shells
That speak seven seas,
Eternal waters away
From the cities of nine
Days' night whose towers will catch   20
In the religious wind
Like stalks of tall, dry straw,
At poor peace I sing
To you strangers (though song
Is a burning and crested act,   25
The fire of birds in
The world's turning wood,
For my sawn, splay sounds),
Out of these seathumbed leaves
That will fly and fall   30
Like leaves of trees and as soon
Crumble and undie

Into the dogdayed night.
Seaward the salmon, sucked sun slips,
And the dumb swans drub blue   35
My dabbed bay's dusk, as I hack
This rumpus of shapes
For you to know
How I, a spinning man,
Glory also this star, bird   40
Roared, sea born, man torn, blood best.
Hark: I trumpet the place,
From fish to jumping hill! Look:
I build my bellowing ark
To the best of my love   45
As the flood begins,
Out of the fountainhead
Of fear, rage red, manalive,
Molten and mountainous to stream
Over the wound asleep   50
Sheep white hollow farms

To Wales in my arms.
Hoo, there, in castle keep,
You king singsong owls, who moonbeam
The flickering runs and dive   55
The dingle furred deer dead!
Huloo, on plumbed bryns,
O my ruffled ring dove
In the hooting, nearly dark
With Welsh and reverent rook,   60
Coo rooing the woods' praise,
Who moons her blue notes from her nest
Down to the curlew herd!
Ho, hullaballoing clan
Agape, with woe   65
In your beaks, on the gabbing capes!
Heigh, on horseback hill, jack

Whisking hare! who
Hears, there, this fox light, my flood ship's
Clangour as I hew and smite   70
(A clash of anvils for my
Hubbub and fiddle, this tune
On a tongued puffball)
But animals thick as thieves
On God's rough tumbling grounds   75
(Hail to His beasthood).
Beasts who sleep good and thin,
Hist, in hogsback woods! The haystacked
Hollow farms in a throng
Of waters cluck and cling,   80
And barnroofs cockcrow war!
O kingdom of neighbours, finned
Felled and quilled, flash to my patch
Work art and the moonshine
Drinking Noah of the bay,   85
With pelt, and scale, and fleece:
Only the drowned deep bells
Of sheep and churches noise
Poor peace as the sun sets
And dark shoals every holy field.   90
We will ride out alone, and then,
Under the stars of Wales,
Cry, Multitudes of arks! Across
The water lidded lands,
Manned with their loves they'll move,   95
Like wooden islands, hill to hill.
Huloo, my proud dove with a flute!
Ahoy, old, sea-legged fox,
Tom tit and Dai mouse!
My ark sings in the sun   100
At God speeded summer's end
And the flood flowers now.

2

BEING BUT MEN

Being but men, we walked into the trees
Afraid, letting our syllables be soft
For fear of waking the rooks,
For fear of coming
Noiselessly into a world of wings and cries.   5

If we were children we might climb,
Catch the rooks sleeping, and break no twig,
And, after the soft ascent,
Thrust out our heads above the branches
To wonder at the unfailing stars.   10

Out of confusion, as the way is,
And the wonder that man knows,
Out of the chaos would come bliss.

That, then, is loveliness, we said,
Children in wonder watching the stars,   15
Is the aim and the end.

Being but men, we walked into the trees.

3

OUT OF THE SIGHS

Out of the sighs a little comes,
But not of grief, for I have knocked down that
Before the agony; the spirit grows,
Forgets, and cries;
A little comes, is tasted and found good;   5

All could not disappoint;
There must, be praised, some certainty,
If not of loving well, then not,
And that is true after perpetual defeat.

After such fighting as the weakest know,   10
There's more than dying;
Lose the great pains or stuff the wound,
He'll ache too long
Through no regret of leaving woman waiting
For her soldier stained with spilt words   15
That spill such acrid blood.

Were that enough, enough to ease the pain,
Feeling regret when this is wasted
That made me happy in the sun,
And, sleeping, made me dream   20
How much was happy while it lasted,
Were vagueness enough and the sweet lies plenty,
The hollow words could bear all suffering.
And cure me of ills.

Were that enough, bone, blood, and sinew,   25
The twisted brain, the fair-formed loin,
Groping for matter under the dog's plate,
Man should be cured of distemper.
For all there is to give I offer:
Crumbs, barn, and halter.   30

4

OUT OF A WAR OF WITS

Out of a war of wits, when folly of words
Was the world's to me, and syllables
Fell hard as whips on an old wound,

My brain came crying into the fresh light,
Called for confessor but there was none
To purge after the wits' fight,
And I was struck dumb by the sun.
Praise that my body be whole, I've limbs,
Not stumps, after the hour of battle,
For the body's brittle and the skin's white.
Praise that only the wits are hurt after the wits' fight.
Overwhelmed by the sun, with a torn brain
I stand beneath the clouds' confessional,
But the hot beams rob me of speech,
After the perils of friends' talk
Reach asking arms up to the milky sky,
After a volley of questions and replies
Lift wit-hurt head for sun to sympathize,
And the sun heals, closing sore eyes.
It is good that the sun shine,
And, after it has sunk, the sane moon,
For out of a house of matchboard and stone
Where men would argue till the stars be green,
It is good to step onto the earth, alone,
And be struck dumb, if only for a time.

5

THEIR FACES SHONE UNDER SOME RADIANCE

Their faces shone under some radiance
Of mingled moonlight and lamplight
That turned the empty kisses into meaning,
The island of such penny love
Into a costly country, the graves
That neighboured them to wells of warmth,
(And skeletons had sap). One minute
Their faces shone; the midnight rain

Hung pointed in the wind,
Before the moon shifted and the sap ran out,   10
She, in her cheap frock, saying some cheap thing,
And he replying,
Not knowing radiance came and passed.
The suicides parade again, now ripe for dying.

6

EARS IN THE TURRETS HEAR

Ears in the turrets hear
Hands grumble on the door,
Eyes in the gables see
The fingers at the locks.
Shall I unbolt or stay   5
Alone till the day I die
Unseen by stranger-eyes
In this white house?
Hands, hold you poison or grapes?

Beyond this island bound   10
By a thin sea of flesh
And a bone coast,
The land lies out of sound
And the hills out of mind.
No birds or flying fish   15
Disturbs this island's rest.

Ears in this island hear
The wind pass like a fire,
Eyes in this island see
Ships anchor off the bay.   20
Shall I run to the ships

With the wind in my hair,
Or stay till the day I die
And welcome no sailor?
Ships, hold you poison or grapes? 25

Hands grumble on the door,
Ships anchor off the bay,
Rain beats the sand and slates.
Shall I let in the stranger,
Shall I welcome the sailor, 30
Or stay till the day I die?

Hands of the stranger and holds of the ships,
Hold you poison or grapes?

7

THE HAND THAT SIGNED THE PAPER

The hand that signed the paper felled a city;
Five sovereign fingers taxed the breath,
Doubled the globe of dead and halved a country;
These five kings did a king to death.

The mighty hand leads to a sloping shoulder, 5
The finger joints are cramped with chalk;
A goose's quill has put an end to murder
That put an end to talk.

The hand that signed the treaty bred a fever,
And famine grew, and locusts came; 10
Great is the hand that holds dominion over
Man by a scribbled name.

The five kings count the dead but do not soften

The crusted wound nor stroke the brow;
A hand rules pity as a hand rules heaven;   15
Hands have no tears to flow.

8

THAT SANITY BE KEPT

That sanity be kept I sit at open windows,
Regard the sky, make unobtrusive comment on the moon,
Sit at open windows in my shirt,
And let the traffic pass, the signals shine,
The engines run, the brass bands keep in tune,   5
For sanity must be preserved.

Thinking of death, I sit and watch the park
Where children play in all their innocence,
And matrons on the littered grass
Absorb the daily sun.   10

The sweet suburban music from a hundred lawns
Comes softly to my ears. The English mowers mow and mow.

I mark the couples walking arm in arm,
Observe their smiles,
Sweet invitations and inventions,   15
See them lend love illustration
By gesture and grimace.
I watch them curiously, detect beneath the laughs
What stands for grief, a vague bewilderment
At things not turning right.   20

I sit at open windows in my shirt,
Observe, like some Jehovah of the west
What passes by, that sanity be kept.

9

BEFORE I KNOCKED

Before I knocked and flesh let enter,
With liquid hands tapped on the womb,
I who was shapeless as the water
That shaped the Jordan near my home
Was brother to Mnetha's daughter   5
And sister to the fathering worm.

I who was deaf to spring and summer,
Who knew not sun nor moon by name,
Felt thud beneath my flesh's armour,
As yet was in a molten form,   10
The leaden stars, the rainy hammer
Swung by my father from his dome.

I knew the message of the winter,
The darted hail, the childish snow,
And the wind was my sister suitor;   15
Wind in me leaped, the hellborn dew;
My veins flowed with the Eastern weather;
Ungotten I knew night and day.

As yet ungotten, I did suffer;
The rack of dreams my lily bones   20
Did twist into a living cipher,
And flesh was snipped to cross the lines
Of gallow crosses on the liver
And brambles in the wringing brains.

My throat knew thirst before the structure   25
Of skin and vein around the well
Where words and water make a mixture
Unfailing till the blood runs foul;

My heart knew love, my belly hunger;
I smelt the maggot in my stool.   30

And time cast forth my mortal creature
To drift or drown upon the seas
Acquainted with the salt adventure
Of tides that never touch the shores.
I who was rich was made the richer   35
By sipping at the vine of days.

I, born of flesh and ghost, was neither
A ghost nor man, but mortal ghost.
And I was struck down by death's feather.
I was a mortal to the last   40
Long breath that carried to my father
The message of his dying christ.

You who bow down at cross and altar,
Remember me and pity Him
Who took my flesh and bone for armour   45
And doublecrossed my mother's womb.

10

SONG

Love me, not as the dreaming nurses
My falling lungs, nor as the cypress
In his age the lass's clay.
Love me and lift your mask.

Love me, not as the girls of heaven   5
Their airy lovers, nor the mermaiden
Her salty lovers in the sea.
Love me and lift your mask.

[33   ]

Love me, not as the ruffling pigeon
The tops of trees, nor as the legion   10
Of the gulls the lip of waves.
Love me and lift your mask.

Love me, as loves the mole his darkness
And the timid deer the tigress:
Hate and fear be your two loves.   15
Love me and lift your mask.

II

THE FORCE THAT THROUGH THE GREEN FUSE
DRIVES THE FLOWER

The force that through the green fuse drives the flower
Drives my green age; that blasts the roots of trees
Is my destroyer.
And I am dumb to tell the crooked rose
My youth is bent by the same wintry fever.   5

The force that drives the water through the rocks
Drives my red blood; that dries the mouthing streams
Turns mine to wax.
And I am dumb to mouth unto my veins
How at the mountain spring the same mouth sucks.   10

The hand that whirls the water in the pool
Stirs the quicksand; that ropes the blowing wind
Hauls my shroud sail.
And I am dumb to tell the hanging man
How of my clay is made the hangman's lime.   15

The lips of time leech to the fountain head;
Love drips and gathers, but the fallen blood
Shall calm her sores.

[34   ]

And I am dumb to tell a weather's wind
How time has ticked a heaven round the stars.   20

And I am dumb to tell the lover's tomb
How at my sheet goes the same crooked worm.

12

LIGHT BREAKS WHERE NO SUN SHINES

Light breaks where no sun shines;
Where no sea runs, the waters of the heart
Push in their tides;
And, broken ghosts with glow-worms in their heads,
The things of light   5
File through the flesh where no flesh decks the bones.

A candle in the thighs
Warms youth and seed and burns the seeds of age;
Where no seed stirs,
The fruit of man unwrinkles in the stars,   10
Bright as a fig;
Where no wax is, the candle shows its hairs.

Dawn breaks behind the eyes;
From poles of skull and toe the windy blood
Slides like a sea;   15
Nor fenced, nor staked, the gushers of the sky
Spout to the rod
Divining in a smile the oil of tears.

Night in the sockets rounds,
Like some pitch moon, the limit of the globes;   20
Day lights the bone;
Where no cold is, the skinning gales unpin
The winter's robes;
The film of spring is hanging from the lids.

[35]

Light breaks on secret lots,   25
On tips of thought where thoughts smell in the rain;
When logics die,
The secret of the soil grows through the eye,
And blood jumps in the sun;
Above the waste allotments the dawn halts.   30

13

A LETTER TO MY AUNT
DISCUSSING THE CORRECT APPROACH TO MODERN
POETRY

To you, my aunt, who would explore
The literary Chankley Bore,
The paths are hard, for you are not
A literary Hottentot
But just a kind and cultured dame   5
Who knows not Eliot (to her shame).
Fie on you, aunt, that you should see
No genius in David G.,
No elemental form and sound
In T.S.E. and Ezra Pound.   10
Fie on you, aunt! I'll show you how
To elevate your middle brow,
And how to scale and see the sights
From modernist Parnassian heights.

First buy a hat, no Paris model   15
But one the Swiss wear when they yodel,
A bowler thing with one or two
Feathers to conceal the view;
And then in sandals walk the street
(All modern painters use their feet   20
For painting, on their canvas strips,
Their wives or mothers minus hips).

Perhaps it would be best if you
Created something very new,
A dirty novel done in Erse   25
Or written backwards in Welsh verse,
Or paintings on the backs of vests,
Or Sanskrit psalms on lepers' chests.
But if this proved imposs-i-ble
Perhaps it would be just as well,   30
For you could then write what you please,
And modern verse is done with ease.

Do not forget that 'limpet' rhymes
With 'strumpet' in these troubled times,
And commas are the worst of crimes;   35
Few understand the works of Cummings,
And few James Joyce's mental slummings,
And few young Auden's coded chatter;
But then it is the few that matter.
Never be lucid, never state,   40
If you would be regarded great,
The simplest thought or sentiment,
(For thought, we know, is decadent);
Never omit such vital words
As belly, genitals, and ——,   45
For these are things that play a part
(And what a part) in all good art.
Remember this: each rose is wormy,
And every lovely woman's germy;
Remember this: that love depends   50
On how the Gallic letter bends;
Remember, too, that life is hell
And even heaven has a smell
Of putrefying angels who
Make deadly whoopee in the blue.   55
These things remembered, what can stop

A poet going to the top?

A final word: before you start
The convulsions of your art,
Remove your brains, take out your heart;   60
Minus these curses, you can be
A genius like David G.

Take courage, aunt, and send your stuff
To Geoffrey Grigson with my luff,
And may I yet live to admire   65
How well your poems light the fire.

14

THIS BREAD I BREAK

This bread I break was once the oat,
This wine upon a foreign tree
Plunged in its fruit;
Man in the day or wind at night
Laid the crops low, broke the grape's joy.   5

Once in this wine the summer blood
Knocked in the flesh that decked the vine,
Once in this bread
The oat was merry in the wind;
Man broke the sun, pulled the wind down.   10

This flesh you break, this blood you let
Make desolation in the vein,
Were oat and grape
Born of the sensual root and sap;
My wine you drink, my bread you snap.   15

15

WHERE ONCE THE WATERS OF YOUR FACE

Where once the waters of your face
Spun to my screws, your dry ghost blows,
The dead turns up its eye;
Where once the mermen through your ice
Pushed up their hair, the dry wind steers   5
Through salt and root and roe.

Where once your green knots sank their splice
Into the tided cord, there goes
The green unraveller,
His scissors oiled, his knife hung loose   10
To cut the channels at their source
And lay the wet fruits low.

Invisible, your clocking tides
Break on the lovebeds of the weeds;
The weed of love's left dry;   15
There round about your stones the shades
Of children go who, from their voids,
Cry to the dolphined sea.

Dry as a tomb, your coloured lids
Shall not be latched while magic glides   20
Sage on the earth and sky;
There shall be corals in your beds,
There shall be serpents in your tides,
Till all our sea-faiths die.

16

I SEE THE BOYS OF SUMMER

I

I see the boys of summer in their ruin
Lay the gold tithings barren,
Setting no store by harvest, freeze the soils;
There in their heat the winter floods
Of frozen loves they fetch their girls,   5
And drown the cargoed apples in their tides.

These boys of light are curdlers in their folly,
Sour the boiling honey;
The jacks of frost they finger in the hives;
There in the sun the frigid threads   10
Of doubt and dark they feed their nerves;
The signal moon is zero in their voids.

I see the summer children in their mothers
Split up the brawned womb's weathers,
Divide the night and day with fairy thumbs;   15
There in the deep with quartered shades
Of sun and moon they paint their dams
As sunlight paints the shelling of their heads.

I see that from these boys shall men of nothing
Stature by seedy shifting,   20
Or lame the air with leaping from its heats;
There from their hearts the dogdayed pulse
Of love and light bursts in their throats.
O see the pulse of summer in the ice.

II

But seasons must be challenged or they totter   25
Into a chiming quarter

Where, punctual as death, we ring the stars;
There, in his night, the black-tongued bells
The sleepy man of winter pulls,
Nor blows back moon-and-midnight as she blows.   30

We are the dark deniers, let us summon
Death from a summer woman,
A muscling life from lovers in their cramp,
From the fair dead who flush the sea
The bright-eyed worm on Davy's lamp,   35
And from the planted womb the man of straw.

We summer boys in this four-winded spinning,
Green of the seaweeds' iron,
Hold up the noisy sea and drop her birds,
Pick the world's ball of wave and froth   40
To choke the deserts with her tides,
And comb the county gardens for a wreath.

In spring we cross our foreheads with the holly,
Heigh ho the blood and berry,
And nail the merry squires to the trees;   45
Here love's damp muscle dries and dies,
Here break a kiss in no love's quarry.
O see the poles of promise in the boys.

III

I see you boys of summer in your ruin.
Man in his maggot's barren.   50
And boys are full and foreign in the pouch.
I am the man your father was.
We are the sons of flint and pitch.
O see the poles are kissing as they cross.

[41]

17

ESPECIALLY WHEN THE OCTOBER WIND

Especially when the October wind
With frosty fingers punishes my hair,
Caught by the crabbing sun I walk on fire
And cast a shadow crab upon the land,
By the sea's side, hearing the noise of birds,   5
Hearing the raven cough in winter sticks,
My busy heart who shudders as she talks
Sheds the syllabic blood and drains her words.

Shut, too, in a tower of words, I mark
On the horizon walking like the trees   10
The wordy shapes of women, and the rows
Of the star-gestured children in the park.
Some let me make you of the vowelled beeches,
Some of the oaken voices, from the roots
Of many a thorny shire tell you notes,   15
Some let me make you of the water's speeches.

Behind a pot of ferns the wagging clock
Tells me the hour's word, the neural meaning
Flies on the shafted disk, declaims the morning
And tell the windy weather in the cock.   20
Some let me make you of the meadow's signs;
The signal grass that tells me all I know
Breaks with the wormy winter through the eye.
Some let me tell you of the raven's sins.

Especially when the October wind   25
(Some let me make you of autumnal spells,
The spider-tongued, and the loud hill of Wales)
With fists of turnips punishes the land,
Some let me make you of the heartless words.
The heart is drained that, spelling in the scurry   30

[42]

Of chemic blood, warned of the coming fury.
By the sea's side hear the dark-vowelled birds.

18

I HAVE LONGED TO MOVE AWAY

I have longed to move away
From the hissing of the spent lie
And the old terrors' continual cry
Growing more terrible as the day
Goes over the hill into the deep sea;   5
I have longed to move away
From the repetition of salutes,
For there are ghosts in the air
And ghostly echoes on paper,
And the thunder of calls and notes.   10

I have longed to move away but am afraid;
Some life, yet unspent, might explode
Out of the old lie burning on the ground,
And, crackling into the air, leave me half-blind.
Neither by night's ancient fear,   15
The parting of hat from hair,
Pursed lips at the receiver,
Shall I fall to death's feather.
By these I would not care to die,
Half convention and half lie.   20

19

SHOULD LANTERNS SHINE

Should lanterns shine, the holy face,
Caught in an octagon of unaccustomed light,
Would wither up, and any boy of love

Look twice before he fell from grace.
The features in their private dark   5
Are formed of flesh, but let the false day come
And from her lips the faded pigments fall,
The mummy cloths expose an ancient breast.

I have been told to reason by the heart,
But heart, like head, leads helplessly;   10
I have been told to reason by the pulse,
And, when it quickens, alter the actions' pace
Till field and roof lie level and the same
So fast I move defying time, the quiet gentleman
Whose beard wags in Egyptian wind.   15

I have heard many years of telling,
And many years should see some change.

The ball I threw while playing in the park
Has not yet reached the ground.

20

INCARNATE DEVIL

Incarnate devil in a talking snake,
The central plains of Asia in his garden,
In shaping-time the circle stung awake,
In shapes of sin forked out the bearded apple,
And God walked there who was a fiddling warden   5
And played down pardon from the heavens' hill.

When we were strangers to the guided seas,
A handmade moon half holy in a cloud,
The wisemen tell me that the garden gods
Twined good and evil on an eastern tree;   10

And when the moon rose windily it was
Black as the beast and paler than the cross.

We in our Eden knew the secret guardian
In sacred waters that no frost could harden,
And in the mighty mornings of the earth;   15
Hell in a horn of sulphur and the cloven myth,
All heaven in a midnight of the sun,
A serpent fiddled in the shaping-time.

21

WHY EAST WIND CHILLS

Why east wind chills and south wind cools
Shall not be known till windwell dries
And west's no longer drowned
In winds that bring the fruit and rind
Of many a hundred falls;   5
Why silk is soft and the stone wounds
The child shall question all his days,
Why night-time rain and the breast's blood
Both quench his thirst he'll have a black reply.

When cometh Jack Frost? the children ask.   10
Shall they clasp a comet in their fists?
Not till, from high and low, their dust
Sprinkles in children's eyes a long-last sleep
And dusk is crowded with the children's ghosts,
Shall a white answer echo from the rooftops.   15

All things are known: the stars' advice
Calls some content to travel with the winds,

Though what the stars ask as they round
Time upon time the towers of the skies
Is heard but little till the stars go out. 20
I hear content, and 'Be content'
Ring like a handbell through the corridors,
And 'Know no answer', and I know
No answer to the children's cry
Of echo's answer and the man of frost 25
And ghostly comets over the raised fists.

22

HERE IN THIS SPRING

Here in this spring, stars float along the void;
Here in this ornamental winter
Down pelts the naked weather;
This summer buries a spring bird.

Symbols are selected from the years' 5
Slow rounding of four seasons' coasts,
In autumn teach three seasons' fires
And four birds' notes.

I should tell summer from the trees, the worms
Tell, if at all, the winter's storms 10
Or the funeral of the sun;
I should learn spring by the cuckooing,
And the slug should teach me destruction.

A worm tells summer better than the clock,
The slug's a living calendar of days; 15
What shall it tell me if a timeless insect
Says the world wears away?

[46]

AND DEATH SHALL HAVE NO DOMINION

And death shall have no dominion.
Dead men naked they shall be one
With the man in the wind and the west moon;
When their bones are picked clean and the clean bones gone,
They shall have stars at elbow and foot;   5
Though they go mad they shall be sane,
Though they sink through the sea they shall rise again;
Though lovers be lost love shall not;
And death shall have no dominion.

And death shall have no dominion.   10
Under the windings of the sea
They lying long shall not die windily;
Twisting on racks when sinews give way,
Strapped to a wheel, yet they shall not break;
Faith in their hands shall snap in two,   15
And the unicorn evils run them through;
Split all ends up they shan't crack;
And death shall have no dominion.

And death shall have no dominion.
No more may gulls cry at their ears   20
Or waves break loud on the seashores;
Where blew a flower may a flower no more
Lift its head to the blows of the rain;
Though they be mad and dead as nails,
Heads of the characters hammer through daisies;   25
Break in the sun till the sun breaks down,
And death shall have no dominion.

THE SPIRE CRANES

The spire cranes. Its statue is an aviary.
From the stone nest it does not let the feathery
Carved birds blunt their striking throats on the salt gravel,
Pierce the spilt sky with diving wing in weed and heel
An inch in froth. Chimes cheat the prison spire, pelter   5
In time like outlaw rains on that priest, water,
Time for the swimmers' hands, music for silver lock
And mouth. Both note and plume plunge from the spire's hook.
Those craning birds are choice for you, songs that jump back
To the built voice, or fly with winter to the bells,   10
But do not travel down dumb wind like prodigals.

O MAKE ME A MASK

O make me a mask and a wall to shut from your spies
Of the sharp, enamelled eyes and the spectacled claws
Rape and rebellion in the nurseries of my face,
Gag of a dumbstruck tree to block from bare enemies
The bayonet tongue in this undefended prayerpiece,   5
The present mouth, and the sweetly blown trumpet of lies,
Shaped in old armour and oak the countenance of a dunce
To shield the glistening brain and blunt the examiners,
And a tear-stained widower grief drooped from the lashes
To veil belladonna and let the dry eyes perceive   10
Others betray the lamenting lies of their losses
By the curve of the nude mouth or the laugh up the sleeve.

AFTER THE FUNERAL

(In memory of Ann Jones)

After the funeral, mule praises, brays,
Windshake of sailshaped ears, muffle-toed tap
Tap happily of one peg in the thick
Grave's foot, blinds down the lids, the teeth in black,
The spittled eyes, the salt ponds in the sleeves,   5
Morning smack of the spade that wakes up sleep,
Shakes a desolate boy who slits his throat
In the dark of the coffin and sheds dry leaves,
That breaks one bone to light with a judgment clout,
After the feast of tear-stuffed time and thistles   10
In a room with a stuffed fox and a stale fern,
I stand, for this memorial's sake, alone
In the snivelling hours with dead, humped Ann
Whose hooded, fountain heart once fell in puddles
Round the parched worlds of Wales and drowned each sun   15
(Though this for her is a monstrous image blindly
Magnified out of praise; her death was a still drop;
She would not have me sinking in the holy
Flood of her heart's fame; she would lie dumb and deep
And need no druid of her broken body).   20
But I, Ann's bard on a raised hearth, call all
The seas to service that her wood-tongued virtue
Babble like a bellbuoy over the hymning heads,
Bow down the walls of the ferned and foxy woods
That her love sing and swing through a brown chapel,   25
Bless her bent spirit with four, crossing birds.
Her flesh was meek as milk, but this skyward statue
With the wild breast and blessed and giant skull
Is carved from her in a room with a wet window
In a fiercely mourning house in a crooked year.   30

I know her scrubbed and sour humble hands
Lie with religion in their cramp, her threadbare
Whisper in a damp word, her wits drilled hollow,
Her fist of a face died clenched on a round pain;
And sculptured Ann is seventy years of stone.   35
These cloud-sopped, marble hands, this monumental
Argument of the hewn voice, gesture and psalm,
Storm me forever over her grave until
The stuffed lung of the fox twitch and cry Love
And the strutting fern lay seeds on the black sill.   40

27

WHEN ALL MY FIVE AND COUNTRY SENSES SEE

When all my five and country senses see,
The fingers will forget green thumbs and mark
How, through the halfmoon's vegetable eye,
Husk of young stars and handfull zodiac,
Love in the frost is pared and wintered by,   5
The whispering ears will watch love drummed away
Down breeze and shell to a discordant beach,
And, lashed to syllables, the lynx tongue cry
That her fond wounds are mended bitterly.
My nostrils see her breath burn like a bush.   10

My one and noble heart has witnesses
In all love's countries, that will grope awake;
And when blind sleep drops on the spying senses,
The heart is sensual, though five eyes break.

28

THE TOMBSTONE TOLD WHEN SHE DIED

The tombstone told when she died.
Her two surnames stopped me still.

A virgin married at rest.
She married in this pouring place,
That I struck one day by luck,   5
Before I heard in my mother's side
Or saw in the looking-glass shell
The rain through her cold heart speak
And the sun killed in her face.
More the thick stone cannot tell.   10

Before she lay on a stranger's bed
With a hand plunged through her hair,
Or that rainy tongue beat back
Through the devilish years and innocent deaths
To the room of a secret child,   15
Among men later I heard it said
She cried her white-dressed limbs were bare
And her red lips were kissed black,
She wept in her pain and made mouths,
Talked and tore though her eyes smiled.   20

I who saw in a hurried film
Death and this mad heroine
Meet once on a mortal wall,
Heard her speak through the chipped beak
Of the stone bird guarding her: 25
I died before bedtime came
But my womb was bellowing
And I felt with my bare fall
A blazing red harsh head tear up
And the dear floods of his hair.   30

29

ON NO WORK OF WORDS

On no work of words now for three lean months in the bloody

Belly of the rich year and the big purse of my body
I bitterly take to task my poverty and craft:

To take to give is all, return what is hungrily given
Puffing the pounds of manna up through the dew to heaven,   5
The lovely gift of the gab bangs back on a blind shaft.

To lift to leave from the treasures of man is pleasing death
That will rake at last all currencies of the marked breath
And count the taken, forsaken mysteries in a bad dark.

To surrender now is to pay the expensive ogre twice.   10
Ancient woods of my blood, dash down to the nut of the seas
If I take to burn or return this world which is each man's work.

30

TWENTY-FOUR YEARS

Twenty-four years remind the tears of my eyes.
(Bury the dead for fear that they walk to the grave in labour.)
In the groin of the natural doorway I crouched like a tailor
Sewing a shroud for a journey
By the light of the meat-eating sun.
Dressed to die, the sensual strut begun,   5
With my red veins full of money,
In the final direction of the elementary town
I advance for as long as forever is.

31

ONCE IT WAS THE COLOUR OF SAYING

Once it was the colour of saying
Soaked my table the uglier side of a hill
With a capsized field where a school sat still

And a black and white patch of girls grew playing;
The gentle seaslides of saying I must undo   5
That all the charmingly drowned arise to cockcrow and kill.
When I whistled with mitching boys through a reservoir park
Where at night we stoned the cold and cuckoo
Lovers in the dirt of their leafy beds,
The shade of their trees was a word of many shades   10
And a lamp of lightning for the poor in the dark;
Now my saying shall be my undoing,
And every stone I wind off like a reel.

32

'IF MY HEAD HURT A HAIR'S FOOT'

'If my head hurt a hair's foot
Pack back the downed bone. If the unpricked ball of my breath
Bump on a spout let the bubbles jump out.
Sooner drop with the worm of the ropes round my throat
Than bully ill love in the clouted scene.   5

'All game phrases fit your ring of a cockfight:
I'll comb the snared woods with a glove on a lamp,
Peck, sprint, dance on fountains and duck time
Before I rush in a crouch the ghost with a hammer, air,
Strike light, and bloody a loud room.   10

'If my bunched, monkey coming is cruel
Rage me back to the making house. My hand unravel
When you sew the deep door. The bed is a cross place.
Bend, if my journey ache, direction like an arc or make
A limp and riderless shape to leap nine thinning months.'   15

'No. Not for Christ's dazzling bed
Or a nacreous sleep among soft particles and charms
My dear would I change my tears or your iron head.

[53   ]

Thrust, my daughter or son, to escape, there is none, none, none,
Nor when all ponderous heaven's host of waters breaks.   20

'Now to awake husked of gestures and my joy like a cave
To the anguish and carrion, to the infant forever unfree,
O my lost love bounced from a good home;
The grain that hurries this way from the rim of the grave
Has a voice and a house, and there and here you must couch   25
    and cry.

'Rest beyond choice in the dust-appointed grain,
At the breast stored with seas. No return
Through the waves of the fat streets nor the skeleton's thin ways.
The grave and my calm body are shut to your coming as stone,
And the endless beginning of prodigies suffers open.'   30

33

TO OTHERS THAN YOU

Friend by enemy I call you out.

You with a bad coin in your socket,
You my friend there with a winning air
Who palmed the lie on me when you looked
Brassily at my shyest secret,   5
Enticed with twinkling bits of the eye
Till the sweet tooth of my love bit dry,
Rasped at last, and I stumbled and sucked,
Whom now I conjure to stand as thief
In the memory worked by mirrors,   10
With unforgettably smiling act,
Quickness of hand in the velvet glove
And my whole heart under your hammer,
Were once such a creature, so gay and frank
A desireless familiar   15

[54]

I never thought to utter or think
While you displaced a truth in the air,

That though I loved them for their faults
As much as for their good,
My friends were enemies on stilts   20
With their heads in a cunning cloud.

34

PAPER AND STICKS

Paper and sticks and shovel and match
Why won't the news of the old world catch
And the fire in a temper start

Once I had a rich boy for myself
I loved his body and his navy blue wealth   5
And I lived in his purse and his heart

When in our bed I was tossing and turning
All I could see were his brown eyes burning
By the green of a one pound note

I talk to him as I clean the grate   10
O my dear it's never too late
To take me away as you whispered and wrote

I had a handsome and well-off boy
I'll share my money and we'll run for joy
With a bouncing and silver spooned kid   15

Sharp and shrill my silly tongue scratches
Words on the air as the fire catches
You never did and *he* never did.

WHEN I WOKE

When I woke, the town spoke.
Birds and clocks and cross bells
Dinned aside the coiling crowd,
The reptile profligates in a flame,
Spoilers and pokers of sleep,   5
The next-door sea dispelled
Frogs and satans and woman-luck,
While a man outside with a billhook,
Up to his head in his blood,
Cutting the morning off,   10
The warm-veined double of Time
And his scarving beard from a book,
Slashed down the last snake as though
It were a wand or subtle bough,
Its tongue peeled in the wrap of a leaf.   15

Every morning I make,
God in bed, good and bad,
After a water-face walk,
The death-stagged scatter-breath
Mammoth and sparrowfall   20
Everybody's earth.
Where birds ride like leaves and boats like ducks
I heard, this morning, waking,
Crossly out of the town noises
A voice in the erected air,   25
No prophet-progeny of mine,
Cry my sea town was breaking.
No Time, spoke the clocks, no God, rang the bells,
I drew the white sheet over the islands
And the coins on my eyelids sang like shells.   30

THERE WAS A SAVIOUR

There was a saviour
Rarer than radium,
Commoner than water, crueller than truth;
Children kept from the sun
Assembled at his tongue   5
To hear the golden note turn in a groove,
Prisoners of wishes locked in their eyes
In the jails and studies of his keyless smiles.

The voice of children says
From a lost wilderness   10
There was calm to be done in his safe unrest,
When hindering man hurt
Man, animal, or bird
We hid our fears in that murdering breath,
Silence, silence to do, when earth grew loud,   15
In lairs and asylums of the tremendous shout.

There was glory to hear
In the churches of his tears,
Under his downy arm you sighed as he struck,
O you who could not cry   20
On to the ground when a man died
Put a tear for joy in the unearthly flood
And laid your cheek against a cloud-formed shell:
Now in the dark there is only yourself and myself.

Two proud, blacked brothers cry,   25
Winter-locked side by side,
To this inhospitable hollow year,
O we who could not stir
One lean sigh when we heard

Greed on man beating near and fire neighbour   30
But wailed and nested in the sky-blue wall
Now break a giant tear for the little known fall,

        For the drooping of homes
        That did not nurse our bones,
    Brave deaths of only ones but never found,   35
        Now see, alone in us,
        Our own true strangers' dust
    Ride through the doors of our unentered house.
Exiled in us we arouse the soft,
Unclenched, armless, silk and rough love that breaks all rocks. 40

37

ON THE MARRIAGE OF A VIRGIN

Waking alone in a multitude of loves when morning's light
Surprised in the opening of her nightlong eyes
His golden yesterday asleep upon the iris
And this day's sun leapt up the sky out of her thighs
Was miraculous virginity old as loaves and fishes,   5
Though the moment of a miracle is unending lightning
And the shipyards of Galilee's footprints hide a navy of doves.

No longer will the vibrations of the sun desire on
Her deepsea pillow where once she married alone,
Her heart all ears and eyes, lips catching the avalanche   10
Of the golden ghost who ringed with his streams her mercury bone,
Who under the lids of her windows hoisted his golden luggage,
For a man sleeps where fire leapt down and she learns through his
    arm
That other sun, the jealous coursing of the unrivalled blood.

THE HUNCHBACK IN THE PARK

The hunchback in the park
A solitary mister
Propped between trees and water
From the opening of the garden lock
That lets the trees and water enter   5
Until the Sunday sombre bell at dark

Eating bread from a newspaper
Drinking water from the chained cup
That the children filled with gravel
In the fountain basin where I sailed my ship   10
Slept at night in a dog kennel
But nobody chained him up.

Like the park birds he came early
Like the water he sat down
And Mister they called Hey mister   15
The truant boys from the town
Running when he had heard them clearly
On out of sound

Past lake and rockery
Laughing when he shook his paper   20
Hunchbacked in mockery
Through the loud zoo of the willow groves
Dodging the park keeper
With his stick that picked up leaves.

And the old dog sleeper   25
Alone between nurses and swans
While the boys among willows

Made the tigers jump out of their eyes
To roar on the rockery stones
And the groves were blue with sailors   30

Made all day until bell time
A woman figure without fault
Straight as a young elm
Straight and tall from his crooked bones
That she might stand in the night   35
After the locks and chains

All night in the unmade park
After the railings and shrubberies
The birds the grass the trees the lake
And the wild boys innocent as strawberries   40
Had followed the hunchback
To his kennel in the dark.

39

AMONG THOSE KILLED IN THE DAWN RAID WAS A MAN AGED A HUNDRED

When the morning was waking over the war
He put on his clothes and stepped out and he died,
The locks yawned loose and a blast blew them wide,
He dropped where he loved on the burst pavement stone
And the funeral grains of the slaughtered floor.   5
Tell his street on its back he stopped a sun
And the craters of his eyes grew springshoots and fire
When all the keys shot from the locks, and rang.
Dig no more for the chains of his grey-haired heart.
The heavenly ambulance drawn by a wound   10
Assembling waits for the spade's ring on the cage.
O keep his bones away from that common cart,
The morning is flying on the wings of his age
And a hundred storks perch on the sun's right hand.

CEREMONY AFTER A FIRE RAID

I

Myselves
The grievers
Grieve
Among the street burned to tireless death
A child of a few hours   5
With its kneading mouth
Charred on the black breast of the grave
The mother dug, and its arms full of fires.

Begin
With singing   10
Sing
Darkness kindled back into beginning
When the caught tongue nodded blind,
A star was broken
Into the centuries of the child   15
Myselves grieve now, and miracles cannot atone.

Forgive
Us forgive
Give
Us your death that myselves the believers   20
May hold it in a great flood
Till the blood shall spurt,
And the dust shall sing like a bird
As the grains blow, as your death grows, through our heart.

Crying   25
Your dying
Cry,
Child beyond cockrow, by the fire-dwarfed

Street we chant the flying sea
In the body bereft.   30
Love is the last light spoken. Oh
Seed of sons in the loin of the black husk left.

II

I know not whether
Adam or Eve, the adorned holy bullock
Or the white ewe lamb   35
Or the chosen virgin
Laid in her snow
On the altar of London,
Was the first to die
In the cinder of the little skull,   40
O bride and bride groom
O Adam and Eve together
Lying in the lull
Under the sad breast of the head stone
White as the skeleton   45
Of the garden of Eden.

I know the legend
Of Adam and Eve is never for a second
Silent in my service
Over the dead infants   50
Over the one
Child who was priest and servants,
Word, singers, and tongue
In the cinder of the little skull,
Who was the serpent's   55
Night fall and the fruit like a sun,
Man and woman undone,
Beginning crumbled back to darkness
Bare as the nurseries
Of the garden of wilderness.   60

Into the organpipes and steeples
Of the luminous cathedrals,
Into the weathercocks' molten mouths
Rippling in twelve-winded circles,
Into the dead clock burning the hour   65
Over the urn of sabbaths
Over the whirling ditch of daybreak
Over the sun's hovel and the slum of fire
And the golden pavements laid in requiems,
Into the bread in a wheatfield of flames,   70
Into the wine burning like brandy,
The masses of the sea
The masses of the sea under
The masses of the infant-bearing sea
Erupt, fountain, and enter to utter for ever   75
Glory glory glory
The sundering ultimate kingdom of genesis' thunder.

41

LAST NIGHT I DIVED MY BEGGAR ARM

Last night I dived my beggar arm
Days deep in her breast that wore no heart
For me alone but only a rocked drum
Telling the heart I broke of a good habit

That her loving, unfriendly limbs   5
Would plunge my betrayal from sheet to sky
So the betrayed might learn in the sun beams
Of the death in a bed in another country.

POEM

Your breath was shed
Invisible to make
About the soiled undead
Night for my sake,

A raining trail   5
Intangible to them
With biter's tooth and tail
And cobweb drum,

A dark as deep
My love as a round wave   10
To hide the wolves of sleep
And mask the grave.

—

POEM IN OCTOBER

It was my thirtieth year to heaven
Woke to my hearing from harbour and neighbour wood
  And the mussel pooled and the heron
        Priested shore
    The morning beckon   5
With water praying and call of seagull and rook
And the knock of sailing boats on the net webbed wall
    Myself to set foot
        That second
  In the still sleeping town and set forth.   10

My birthday began with the water-
Birds and the birds of the winged trees flying my name
  Above the farms and the white horses
      And I rose
    In the rainy autumn   15
And walked abroad in a shower of all my days.
High tide and the heron dived when I took the road
      Over the border
      And the gates
  Of the town closed as the town awoke.   20

  A springful of larks in a rolling
Cloud and the roadside bushes brimming with whistling
  Blackbirds and the sun of October
      Summery
    On the hill's shoulder,   25
Here were fond climates and sweet singers suddenly
Come in the morning where I wandered and listened
      To the rain wringing
      Wind blow cold
  In the wood faraway under me.   30

  Pale rain over the dwindling harbour
And over the sea wet church the size of a snail
  With its horns through mist and the castle
      Brown as owls
    But all the gardens   35
Of spring and summer were blooming in the tall tales
Beyond the border and under the lark full cloud.
    There could I marvel
      My birthday
Away but the weather turned around.   40

  It turned away from the blithe country
And down the other air and the blue altered sky

Streamed again a wonder of summer
        With apples
    Pears and red currants   45
And I saw in the turning so clearly a child's
Forgotten mornings when he walked with his mother
        Through the parables
            Of sun light
    And the legends of the green chapels   50

    And the twice told fields of infancy
That his tears burned my cheeks and his heart moved in mine.
    These were the woods the river and sea
        Where a boy
        In the listening   55
Summertime of the dead whispered the truth of his joy
To the trees and the stones and the fish in the tide.
        And the mystery
            Sang alive
    Still in the water and singingbirds.   60

    And there could I marvel my birthday
Away but the weather turned around. And the true
    Joy of the long dead child sang burning
        In the sun.
        It was my thirtieth   65
Year to heaven stood there then in the summer noon
Though the town below lay leaved with October blood.
        O may my heart's truth
            Still be sung
    On this high hill in a year's turning.   70

[66   ]

44

HOLY SPRING

O

Out of a bed of love
When that immortal hospital made one more move to soothe
    The cureless counted body,
        And ruin and his causes   5
Over the barbed and shooting sea assumed an army
        And swept into our wounds and houses,
I climb to greet the war in which I have no heart but only
    That one dark I owe my light,
Call for confessor and wiser mirror but there is none   10
    To glow after the god stoning night
And I am struck as lonely as a holy maker by the sun.

No

    Praise that the spring time is all
Gabriel and radiant shrubbery as the morning grows joyful   15
    Out of the woebegone pyre
And the multitude's sultry tear turns cool on the weeping wall,
    My arising prodigal
Sun the father his quiver full of the infants of pure fire,
        But blessed be hail and upheaval   20
That uncalm still it is sure alone to stand and sing
    Alone in the husk of man's home
And the mother and toppling house of the holy spring,
    If only for a last time.

45

THE CONVERSATION OF PRAYER

The conversation of prayers about to be said
By the child going to bed and the man on the stairs

Who climbs to his dying love in her high room,
The one not caring to whom in his sleep he will move
And the other full of tears that she will be dead,   5

Turns in the dark on the sound they know will arise
Into the answering skies from the green ground,
From the man on the stairs and the child by his bed.
The sound about to be said in the two prayers
For the sleep in a safe land and the love who dies   10

Will be the same grief flying. Whom shall they calm?
Shall the child sleep unharmed or the man be crying?
The conversation of prayers about to be said
Turns on the quick and the dead, and the man on the stairs
To-night shall find no dying but alive and warm   15

In the fire of his care his love in the high room.
And the child not caring to whom he climbs his prayer
Shall drown in a grief as deep as his true grave,
And mark the dark eyed wave, through the eyes of sleep,
Dragging him up the stairs to one who lies dead.   20

46

A REFUSAL TO MOURN THE DEATH, BY FIRE, OF A CHILD IN LONDON

Never until the mankind making
Bird beast and flower
Fathering and all humbling darkness
Tells with silence the last light breaking
And the still hour   5
Is come of the sea tumbling in harness

And I must enter again the round
Zion of the water bead

And the synagogue of the ear of corn
Shall I let pray the shadow of a sound   10
Or sow my salt seed
In the least valley of sackcloth to mourn

The majesty and burning of the child's death.
I shall not murder
The mankind of her going with a grave truth   15
Nor blaspheme down the stations of the breath
With any further
Elegy of innocence and youth.

Deep with the first dead lies London's daughter,
Robed in the long friends,   20
The grains beyond age, the dark veins of her mother,
Secret by the unmourning water
Of the riding Thames.
After the first death, there is no other.

47

THIS SIDE OF THE TRUTH
(for Llewelyn)

This side of the truth,
You may not see, my son,
King of your blue eyes
In the blinding country of youth,
That all is undone,   5
Under the unminding skies,
Of innocence and guilt
Before you move to make
One gesture of the heart or head,
Is gathered and spilt   10
Into the winding dark
Like the dust of the dead.

Good and bad, two ways
Of moving about your death
By the grinding sea,   15
King of your heart in the blind days,
Blow away like breath,
Go crying through you and me
And the souls of all men
Into the innocent   20
Dark, and the guilty dark, and good
Death, and bad death, and then
In the last element
Fly like the stars' blood,

Like the sun's tears,   25
Like the moon's seed, rubbish
And fire, the flying rant
Of the sky, king of your six years.
And the wicked wish,
Down the beginning of plants   30
And animals and birds,
Water and light, the earth and sky,
Is cast before you move,
And all your deeds and words,
Each truth, each lie,   35
Die in unjudging love.

48

A WINTER'S TALE

It is a winter's tale
That the snow blind twilight ferries over the lakes
And floating fields from the farm in the cup of the vales,
Gliding windless through the hand folded flakes,
The pale breath of cattle at the stealthy sail,   5

And the stars falling cold,
And the smell of hay in the snow, and the far owl
Warning among the folds, and the frozen hold
Flocked with the sheep white smoke of the farm house cowl
In the river wended vales where the tale was told.   10

Once when the world turned old
On a star of faith pure as the drifting bread,
As the food and flames of the snow, a man unrolled
The scrolls of fire that burned in his heart and head,
Torn and alone in a farm house in a fold   15

Of fields. And burning then
In his firelit island ringed by the winged snow
And the dung hills white as wool and the hen
Roosts sleeping chill till the flame of the cock crow
Combs through the mantled yards and the morning men   20

Stumble out with their spades,
The cattle stirring, the mousing cat stepping shy,
The puffed birds hopping and hunting, the milkmaids
Gentle in their clogs over the fallen sky,
And all the woken farm at its white trades,   25

He knelt, he wept, he prayed,
By the spit and the black pot in the log bright light
And the cup and the cut bread in the dancing shade,
In the muffled house, in the quick of night,
At the point of love, forsaken and afraid.   30

He knelt on the cold stones,
He wept from the crest of grief, he prayed to the veiled sky

May his hunger go howling on bare white bones
Past the statues of the stables and the sky roofed sties
And the duck pond glass and the blinding byres alone   35

    Into the home of prayers
And fires where he should prowl down the cloud
Of his snow blind love and rush in the white lairs.
His naked need struck him howling and bowed
Though no sound flowed down the hand folded air   40

    But only the wind strung
Hunger of birds in the fields of the bread of water, tossed
In high corn and the harvest melting on their tongues.
And his nameless need bound him burning and lost
When cold as snow he should run the wended vales among   45

    The rivers mouthed in night,
And drown in the drifts of his need, and lie curled caught
In the always desiring centre of the white
Inhuman cradle and the bride bed forever sought
By the believer lost and the hurled outcast of light.   50

    Deliver him, he cried,
By losing him all in love, and cast his need
Alone and naked in the engulfing bride,
Never to flourish in the fields of the white seed
Or flower under the time dying flesh astride.   55

    Listen. The minstrels sing
In the departed villages. The nightingale,
Dust in the buried wood, flies on the grains of her wings
And spells on the winds of the dead his winter's tale.
The voice of the dust of water from the withered spring   60

    Is telling. The wizened

[72]

Stream with bells and baying water bounds. The dew rings
On the gristed leaves and the long gone glistening
Parish of snow. The carved mouths in the rock are wind swept
    strings.
Time sings through the intricately dead snow drop. Listen.   65

     It was a hand or sound
In the long ago land that glided the dark door wide
And there outside on the bread of the ground
A she bird rose and rayed like a burning bride.
A she bird dawned, and her breast with snow and scarlet downed. 70

     Look. And the dancers move
On the departed, snow bushed green, wanton in moon light
As a dust of pigeons. Exulting, the graved hooved
Horses, centaur dead, turn and tread the drenched white
Paddocks in the farms of birds. The dead oak walks for love.   75

     The carved limbs in the rock
Leap, as to trumpets. Calligraphy of the old
Leaves is dancing. Lines of age on the stones weave in a flock.
And the harp shaped voice of the water's dust plucks in a fold
Of fields. For love, the long ago she bird rises. Look.   80

     And the wild wings were raised
Above her folded head, and the soft feathered voice
Was flying through the house as though the she bird praised
And all the elements of the snow fall rejoiced
That a man knelt alone in the cup of the vales,   85

     In the mantle and calm,
By the spit and the black pot in the log bright light.
And the sky of birds in the plumed voice charmed
Him up and he ran like a wind after the kindling flight
Past the blind barns and byres of the windless farm.   90

[73]

In the poles of the year
When black birds died like priests in the cloaked hedge row
And over the cloth of counties the far hills rode near,
Under the one leaved trees ran a scarecrow of snow
And fast through the drifts of the thickets antlered like deer, 95

Rags and prayers down the knee-
Deep hillocks and loud on the numbed lakes,
All night lost and long wading in the wake of the she-
Bird through the times and lands and tribes of the slow flakes.
Listen and look where she sails the goose plucked sea, 100

The sky, the bird, the bride,
The cloud, the need, the planted stars, the joy beyond
The fields of seed and the time dying flesh astride,
The heavens, the heaven, the grave, the burning font.
In the far ago land the door of his death glided wide 105

And the bird descended.
On a bread white hill over the cupped farm
And the lakes and floating fields and the river wended
Vales where he prayed to come to the last harm
And the home of prayers and fires, the tale ended. 110

The dancing perishes
On the white, no longer growing green, and, minstrel dead,
The singing breaks in the snow shoed villages of wishes
That once cut the figures of birds on the deep bread
And over the glazed lakes skated the shapes of fishes 115

Flying. The rite is shorn
Of nightingale and centaur dead horse. The springs wither
Back. Lines of age sleep on the stones till trumpeting dawn.
Exultation lies down. Time buries the spring weather
That belled and bounded with the fossil and the dew reborn. 120

For the bird lay bedded
In a choir of wings, as though she slept or died,
And the wings glided wide and he was hymned and wedded,
And through the thighs of the engulfing bride,
The woman breasted and the heaven headed   125

Bird, he was brought low,
Burning in the bride bed of love, in the whirl-
Pool at the wanting centre, in the folds
Of paradise, in the spun bud of the world.
And she rose with him flowering in her melting snow.   130

49

IN MY CRAFT OR SULLEN ART

In my craft or sullen art
Exercised in the still night
When only the moon rages
And the lovers lie abed
With all their griefs in their arms,   5
I labour by singing light
Not for ambition or bread
Or the strut and trade of charms
On the ivory stages
But for the common wages   10
Of their most secret heart.

Not for the proud man apart
From the raging moon I write
On these spindrift pages
Nor for the towering dead   15
With their nightingales and psalms
But for the lovers, their arms

Round the griefs of the ages,
Who pay no praise or wages
Nor heed my craft or art.   20

50

FERN HILL

Now as I was young and easy under the apple boughs
About the lilting house and happy as the grass was green,
　　The night above the dingle starry,
　　　　Time let me hail and climb
　　Golden in the heydays of his eyes,   5
And honoured among wagons I was prince of the apple towns
And once below a time I lordly had the trees and leaves
　　　　Trail with daisies and barley
　　Down the rivers of the windfall light.

And as I was green and carefree, famous among the barns   10
About the happy yard and singing as the farm was home,
　　In the sun that is young once only,
　　　　Time let me play and be
　　Golden in the mercy of his means,
And green and golden I was huntsman and herdsman, the calves 15
Sang to my horn, the foxes on the hills barked clear and cold,
　　　　And the sabbath rang slowly
　　In the pebbles of the holy streams.

All the sun long it was running, it was lovely, the hay
Fields high as the house, the tunes from the chimneys, it was air 20
　　And playing, lovely and watery
　　　　And fire green as grass.
　　And nightly under the simple stars
As I rode to sleep the owls were bearing the farm away,
All the moon long I heard, blessed among stables, the nightjars   25

[76]

Flying with the ricks, and the horses
    Flashing into the dark.

And then to awake, and the farm, like a wanderer white
With the dew, come back, the cock on his shoulder: it was all
    Shining, it was Adam and maiden,   30
       The sky gathered again
    And the sun grew round that very day.
So it must have been after the birth of the simple light
In the first, spinning place, the spellbound horses walking warm
    Out of the whinnying green stable   35
       On to the fields of praise.

And honoured among foxes and pheasants by the gay house
Under the new made clouds and happy as the heart was long,
    In the sun born over and over,
       I ran my heedless ways,   40
    My wishes raced through the house high hay
And nothing I cared, at my sky blue trades, that time allows
In all his tuneful turning so few and such morning songs
    Before the children green and golden
       Follow him out of grace,   45

Nothing I cared, in the lamb white days, that time would take me
Up to the swallow thronged loft by the shadow of my hand,
    In the moon that is always rising,
       Nor that riding to sleep
    I should hear him fly with the high fields   50
And wake to the farm forever fled from the childless land.
Oh as I was young and easy in the mercy of his means,
       Time held me green and dying
    Though I sang in my chains like the sea.

ON A WEDDING ANNIVERSARY

The sky is torn across
This ragged anniversary of two
Who moved for three years in tune
Down the long walks of their vows.

Now their love lies a loss   5
And Love and his patients roar on a chain;
From every true or crater
Carrying cloud, Death strikes their house.

Too late in the wrong rain
They come together whom their love parted: 10
The windows pour into their heart
And the doors burn in their brain.

IN COUNTRY SLEEP

I

Never and never, my girl riding far and near
In the land of the hearthstone tales, and spelled asleep,
Fear or believe that the wolf in a sheepwhite hood
Loping and bleating roughly and blithely shall leap,
My dear, my dear,   5
Out of a lair in the flocked leaves in the dew dipped year
To eat your heart in the house in the rosy wood.

Sleep, good, for ever, slow and deep, spelled rare and wise,
My girl ranging the night in the rose and shire
Of the hobnail tales: no gooseherd or swine will turn   10
Into a homestall king or hamlet of fire

                                        And prince of ice
To court the honeyed heart from your side before sunrise
In a spinney of ringed boys and ganders, spike and burn,

Nor the innocent lie in the rooting dingle wooed   15
And staved, and riven among plumes my rider weep.
From the broomed witch's spume you are shielded by fern
And flower of country sleep and the greenwood keep.
                                        Lie fast and soothed,
Safe be and smooth from the bellows of the rushy brood.   20
Never, my girl, until tolled to sleep by the stern

Bell believe or fear that the rustic shade or spell
Shall harrow and snow the blood while you ride wide and near,
For who unmanningly haunts the mountain ravened eaves
Or skulks in the dell moon but moonshine echoing clear   25
                                        From the starred well?
A hill touches an angel. Out of a saint's cell
The nightbird lauds through nunneries and domes of leaves

Her robin breasted tree, three Marys in the rays.
Sanctum sanctorum the animal eye of the wood   30
In the rain telling its beads, and the gravest ghost
The owl at its knelling. Fox and holt kneel before blood.
                                        Now the tales praise
The star rise at pasture and nightlong the fables graze
On the lord's-table of the bowing grass. Fear most   35

For ever of all not the wolf in his baaing hood
Nor the tusked prince, in the ruttish farm, at the rind
And mire of love, but the Thief as meek as the dew.
The country is holy: O bide in that country kind,
                                        Know the green good, 40
Under the prayer wheeling moon in the rosy wood
Be shielded by chant and flower and gay may you

[79]

Lie in grace. Sleep spelled at rest in the lowly house
In the squirrel nimble grove, under linen and thatch
And star: held and blessed, though you scour the high four   45
Winds, from the dousing shade and the roarer at the latch,
                                        Cool in your vows.
Yet out of the beaked, web dark and the pouncing boughs
Be you sure the Thief will seek a way sly and sure

And sly as snow and meek as dew blown to the thorn,   50
This night and each vast night until the stern bell talks
In the tower and tolls to sleep over the stalls
Of the hearthstone tales my own, lost love; and the soul walks
                                        The waters shorn.
This night and each night since the falling star you were born, 55
Ever and ever he finds a way, as the snow falls,

As the rain falls, hail on the fleece, as the vale mist rides
Through the haygold stalls, as the dew falls on the wind-
Milled dust of the apple tree and the pounded islands
Of the morning leaves, as the star falls, as the winged   60
                                        Apple seed glides,
And falls, and flowers in the yawning wound at our sides,
As the world falls, silent as the cyclone of silence.

II

Night and the reindeer on the clouds above the haycocks
And the wings of the great roc ribboned for the fair!   65
The leaping saga of prayer! And high, there, on the hare-
                                        Heeled winds the rooks
Cawing from their black bethels soaring, the holy books
Of birds! Among the cocks like fire the red fox

Burning! Night and the vein of birds in the winged, sloe wrist   70
Of the wood! Pastoral beat of blood through the laced leaves!

The stream from the priest black wristed spinney and sleeves
Of thistling frost
Of the nightingale's din and tale! The upgiven ghost
Of the dingle torn to singing and the surpliced   75

Hill of cypresses! The din and tale in the skimmed
Yard of the buttermilk rain on the pail! The sermon
Of blood! The bird loud vein! The saga from mermen
To seraphim
Leaping! The gospel rooks! All tell, this night, of him   80
Who comes as red as the fox and sly as the heeled wind.

Illumination of music! The lulled black-backed
Gull, on the wave with sand in its eyes! And the foal moves
Through the shaken greensward lake, silent, on moonshod hooves,
In the winds' wakes. 85
Music of elements, that a miracle makes!
Earth, air, water, fire, singing into the white act,

The haygold haired, my love asleep, and the rift blue
Eyed, in the haloed house, in her rareness and hilly
High riding, held and blessed and true, and so stilly   90
Lying the sky
Might cross its planets, the bell weep, night gather her eyes,
The Thief fall on the dead like the willy nilly dew,

Only for the turning of the earth in her holy
Heart! Slyly, slowly, hearing the wound in her side go   95
Round the sun, he comes to my love like the designed snow,
And truly he
Flows to the strand of flowers like the dew's ruly sea,
And surely he sails like the ship shape clouds. Oh he

Comes designed to my love to steal not her tide raking   100

[81]

Wound, nor her riding high, nor her eyes, nor kindled hair,
But her faith that each vast night and the saga of prayer
                   He comes to take
Her faith that this last night for his unsacred sake
He comes to leave her in the lawless sun awaking   105

Naked and forsaken to grieve he will not come.
Ever and ever by all your vows believe and fear
My dear this night he comes and night without end my dear
                 Since you were born:
And you shall wake, from country sleep, this dawn and each first 110
   dawn,
Your faith as deathless as the outcry of the ruled sun.

53

OVER SIR JOHN'S HILL

Over Sir John's hill,
The hawk on fire hangs still;
In a hoisted cloud, at drop of dusk, he pulls to his claws
And gallows, up the rays of his eyes the small birds of the bay
And the shrill child's play   5
Wars
Of the sparrows and such who swansing, dusk, in wrangling
   hedges.
And blithely they squawk
To fiery tyburn over the wrestle of elms until
The flashed the noosed hawk   10
Crashes, and slowly the fishing holy stalking heron
In the river Towy below bows his tilted headstone.

Flash, and the plumes crack,
And a black cap of jack-
Daws Sir John's just hill dons, and again the gulled birds hare   15

To the hawk on fire, the halter height, over Towy's fins,
In a whack of wind.
There
Where the elegiac fisherbird stabs and paddles
In the pebbly dab-filled   20
Shallow and sedge, and 'dilly dilly', calls the loft hawk,
'Come and be killed,'
I open the leaves of the water at a passage
Of psalms and shadows among the pincered sandcrabs prancing

And read, in a shell,   25
Death clear as a buoy's bell:
All praise of the hawk on fire in hawk-eyed dusk be sung,
When his viperish fuse hangs looped with flames under the brand
Wing, and blest shall
Young   30
Green chickens of the bay and bushes cluck, 'dilly dilly,
Come let us die.'
We grieve as the blithe birds, never again, leave shingle and elm,
The heron and I,
I young Aesop fabling to the near night by the dingle   35
Of eels, saint heron hymning in the shell-hung distant

Crystal harbour vale
Where the sea cobbles sail,
And wharves of water where the walls dance and the white cranes
    stilt.
It is the heron and I, under judging Sir John's elmed   40
Hill, tell-tale the knelled
Guilt
Of the led-astray birds whom God, for their breast of whistles,
Have mercy on,
God in his whirlwind silence save, who marks the sparrows hail,   45
For their souls' song.
Now the heron grieves in the weeded verge. Through windows
Of dusk and water I see the tilting whispering

[83   ]

Heron, mirrored, go,
As the snapt feathers snow,   50
Fishing in the tear of the Towy. Only a hoot owl
Hollows, a grassblade blown in cupped hands, in the looted elms
And no green cocks or hens
Shout
Now on Sir John's hill. The heron, ankling the scaly   55
Lowlands of the waves
Makes all the music; and I who hear the tune of the slow,
Wear-willow river, grave,
Before the lunge of the night, the notes on this time-shaken
Stone for the sake of the souls of the slain birds sailing.   60

54

IN THE WHITE GIANT'S THIGH

Through throats where many rivers meet, the curlews cry,
Under the conceiving moon, on the high chalk hill,
And there this night I walk in the white giant's thigh
Where barren as boulders women lie longing still

To labour and love though they lay down long ago.   5

Through throats where many rivers meet, the women pray,
Pleading in the waded bay for the seed to flow
Though the names on their weed grown stones are rained away,

And alone in the night's eternal, curving act
They yearn with tongues of curlews for the unconceived   10
And immemorial sons of the cudgelling, hacked

Hill. Who once in gooseskin winter loved all ice leaved
In the courters' lanes, or twined in the ox roasting sun
In the wains tonned so high that the wisps of the hay
Clung to the pitching clouds, or gay with any one   15

[84]

Young as they in the after milking moonlight lay

Under the lighted shapes of faith and their moonshade
Petticoats galed high, or shy with the rough riding boys,
Now clasp me to their grains in the gigantic glade,

Who once, green countries since, were a hedgerow of joys.   20

Time by, their dust was flesh the swineherd rooted sly,
Flared in the reek of the wiving sty with the rush
Light of his thighs, spreadeagle to the dunghill sky,
Or with their orchard man in the core of the sun's bush
Rough as cows' tongues and thrashed with brambles their butter-   25
    milk
Manes, under his quenchless summer barbed gold to the bone,

Or rippling soft in the spinney moon as the silk
And ducked and draked white lake that harps to a hail stone.

Who once were a bloom of wayside brides in the hawed house
And heard the lewd, wooed field flow to the coming frost,   30
The scurrying, furred small friars squeal, in the dowse
Of day, in the thistle aisles, till the white owl crossed

Their breast, the vaulting does roister, the horned bucks climb
Quick in the wood at love, where a torch of foxes foams,
All birds and beasts of the linked night uproar and chime   35

And the mole snout blunt under his pilgrimage of domes,
Or, butter fat goosegirls, bounced in a gambo bed,
Their breasts full of honey, under their gander king
Trounced by his wings in the hissing shippen, long dead

[85]

And gone that barley dark where their clogs danced in the spring, 40
And their firefly hairpins flew, and the ricks ran round—

(But nothing bore, no mouthing babe to the veined hives
Hugged, and barren and bare on Mother Goose's ground
They with the simple Jacks were a boulder of wives)—

Now curlew cry me down to kiss the mouths of their dust. 45

The dust of their kettles and clocks swings to and fro
Where the hay rides now or the bracken kitchens rust
As the arc of the billhooks that flashed the hedges low
And cut the birds' boughs that the minstrel sap ran red.
They from houses where the harvest kneels, hold me hard, 50
Who heard the tall bell sail down the Sundays of the dead
And the rain wring out its tongues on the faded yard,
Teach me the love that is evergreen after the fall leaved
Grave, after Belovéd on the grass gulfed cross is scrubbed
Off by the sun and Daughters no longer grieved 55
Save by their long desirers in the fox cubbed
Streets or hungering in the crumbled wood: to these
Hale dead and deathless do the women of the hill
Love for ever meridian through the courters' trees

And the daughters of darkness flame like Fawkes fires still. 60

55

LAMENT

When I was a windy boy and a bit
And the black spit of the chapel fold,
(Sighed the old ram rod, dying of women),
I tiptoed shy in the gooseberry wood,
The rude owl cried like a telltale tit, 5

I skipped in a blush as the big girls rolled
Ninepin down on the donkeys' common,
And on seesaw sunday nights I wooed
Whoever I would with my wicked eyes,
The whole of the moon I could love and leave   10
All the green leaved little weddings' wives
In the coal black bush and let them grieve.

When I was a gusty man and a half
And the black beast of the beetles' pews,
(Sighed the old ram rod, dying of bitches),   15
Not a boy and a bit in the wick-
Dipping moon and drunk as a new dropped calf,
I whistled all night in the twisted flues,
Midwives grew in the midnight ditches,
And the sizzling beds of the town cried, Quick!—   20
Whenever I dove in a breast high shoal,
Wherever I ramped in the clover quilts,
Whatsoever I did in the coal-
Black night, I left my quivering prints.

When I was a man you could call a man   25
And the black cross of the holy house,
(Sighed the old ram rod, dying of welcome),
Brandy and ripe in my bright, bass prime,
No springtailed tom in the red hot town
With every simmering woman his mouse   30
But a hillocky bull in the swelter
Of summer come in his great good time
To the sultry, biding herds, I said,
Oh, time enough when the blood creeps cold,
And I lie down but to sleep in bed,   35
For my sulking, skulking, coal black soul!

When I was a half of the man I was

And serve me right as the preachers warn,
(Sighed the old ram rod, dying of downfall),
No flailing calf or cat in a flame   40
Or hickory bull in milky grass
But a black sheep with a crumpled horn,
At last the soul from its foul mousehole
Slunk pouting out when the limp time came;
And I gave my soul a blind, slashed eye,   45
Gristle and rind, and a roarers' life,
And I shoved it into the coal black sky
To find a woman's soul for a wife.

Now I am a man no more no more
And a black reward for a roaring life,   50
(Sighed the old ram rod, dying of strangers),
Tidy and cursed in my dove cooed room
I lie down thin and hear the good bells jaw—
For, oh, my soul found a sunday wife
In the coal black sky and she bore angels!   55
Harpies around me out of her womb!
Chastity prays for me, piety sings,
Innocence sweetens my last black breath,
Modesty hides my thighs in her wings,
And all the deadly virtues plague my death!   60

56

DO NOT GO GENTLE INTO THAT GOOD NIGHT

Do not go gentle into that good night,
Old age should burn and rave at close of day;
Rage, rage against the dying of the light.

Though wise men at their end know dark is right,
Because their words had forked no lightning they   5
Do not go gentle into that good night.

Good men, the last wave by, crying how bright
Their frail deeds might have danced in a green bay,
Rage, rage against the dying of the light.

Wild men who caught and sang the sun in flight,   10
And learn, too late, they grieved it on its way,
Do not go gentle into that good night.

Grave men, near death, who see with blinding sight
Blind eyes could blaze like meteors and be gay,
Rage, rage against the dying of the light.   15

And you, my father, there on the sad height,
Curse, bless, me now with your fierce tears, I pray.
Do not go gentle into that good night.
Rage, rage against the dying of the light.

57
POEM ON HIS BIRTHDAY

In the mustardseed sun,
By full tilt river and switchback sea
  Where the cormorants scud,
In his house on stilts high among beaks
  And palavers of birds   5
This sandgrain day in the bent bay's grave
  He celebrates and spurns
His driftwood thirty-fifth wind turned age;
  Herons spire and spear.

Under and round him go   10
Flounders, gulls, on their cold, dying trails,
  Doing what they are told,
Curlews aloud in the congered waves
  Work at their ways to death,
And the rhymer in the long tongued room,   15

[89]

Who tolls his birthday bell,
Toils towards the ambush of his wounds;
  Herons, steeple stemmed, bless.

  In the thistledown fall,
He sings towards anguish; finches fly   20
  In the claw tracks of hawks
On a seizing sky; small fishes glide
  Through wynds and shells of drowned
Ship towns to pastures of otters. He
  In his slant, racking house   25
And the hewn coils of his trade perceives
  Herons walk in their shroud,

  The livelong river's robe
Of minnows wreathing around their prayer;
  And far at sea he knows,   30
Who slaves to his crouched, eternal end
  Under a serpent cloud,
Dolphins dive in their turnturtle dust,
  The rippled seals streak down
To kill and their own tide daubing blood   35
  Slides good in the sleek mouth.

  In a cavernous, swung
Wave's silence, wept white angelus knells.
  Thirty-five bells sing struck
On skull and scar where his loves lie wrecked,   40
  Steered by the falling stars.
And to-morrow weeps in a blind cage
  Terror will rage apart
Before chains break to a hammer flame
  And love unbolts the dark

         45

  And freely he goes lost
In the unknown, famous light of great

And fabulous, dear God.
Dark is a way and light is a place,
    Heaven that never was   50
Nor will be ever is always true,
    And, in that brambled void,
Plenty as blackberries in the woods
    The dead grow for His joy.

    There he might wander bare   55
With the spirits of the horseshoe bay
    Or the stars' seashore dead,
Marrow of eagles, the roots of whales
    And wishbones of wild geese,
With blessed, unborn God and His Ghost,   60
    And every soul His priest,
Gulled and chanter in young Heaven's fold
    Be at cloud quaking peace,

    But dark is a long way.
He, on the earth of the night, alone   65
    With all the living, prays,
Who knows the rocketing wind will blow
    The bones out of the hills,
And the scythed boulders bleed, and the last
    Rage shattered waters kick   70
Masts and fishes to the still quick stars,
    Faithlessly unto Him

    Who is the light of old
And air shaped Heaven where souls grow wild
    As horses in the foam: 75
Oh, let me midlife mourn by the shrined
    And druid herons' vows
The voyage to ruin I must run,
    Dawn ships clouted aground,
Yet, though I cry with tumbledown tongue,   80
    Count my blessings aloud:

Four elements and five
Senses, and man a spirit in love
  Tangling through this spun slime
To his nimbus bell cool kingdom come   85
  And the lost, moonshine domes,
And the sea that hides his secret selves
  Deep in its black, base bones,
Lulling of spheres in the seashell flesh,
  And this last blessing most,   90

That the closer I move
To death, one man through his sundered hulks,
  The louder the sun blooms
And the tusked, ramshackling sea exults;
  And every wave of the way   95
And gale I tackle, the whole world then,
  With more triumphant faith
That ever was since the world was said,
  Spins its morning of praise,

I hear the bouncing hills   100
Grow larked and greener at berry brown
  Fall and the dew larks sing
Taller this thunderclap spring, and how
  More spanned with angels ride
The mansouled fiery islands! Oh,   105
  Holier then their eyes,
And my shining men no more alone
  As I sail out to die.

58

ELEGY

Too proud to die, broken and blind he died
The darkest way, and did not turn away,

[92]

A cold kind man brave in his narrow pride

On that darkest day. Oh, forever may
He lie lightly, at last, on the last, crossed   5
Hill, under the grass, in love, and there grow

Young among the long flocks, and never lie lost
Or still all the numberless days of his death, though
Above all he longed for his mother's breast

Which was rest and dust, and in the kind ground   10
The darkest justice of death, blind and unblessed.
Let him find no rest but be fathered and found,

I prayed in the crouching room, by his blind bed,
In the muted house, one minute before
Noon, and night, and light. The rivers of the dead   15

Veined his poor hand I held, and I saw
Through his unseeing eyes to the roots of the sea.
[An old tormented man three-quarters blind,

I am not too proud to cry that He and he
Will never never go out of my mind.   20
All his bones crying, and poor in all but pain,

Being innocent, he dreaded that he died
Hating his God, but what he was was plain:
An old kind man brave in his burning pride.

The sticks of the house were his; his books he owned. 25
Even as a baby he had never cried;
Nor did he now, save to his secret wound.

[93]

Out of his eyes I saw the last light glide.
Here among the light of the lording sky
An old man is with me where I go   30

Walking in the meadows of his son's eye
On whom a world of ills came down like snow.
He cried as he died, fearing at last the spheres'

Last sound, the world going out without a breath:
Too proud to cry, too frail to check the tears,   35
And caught between two nights, blindness and death.

O deepest wound of all that he should die
On that darkest day. Oh, he could hide
The tears out of his eyes, too proud to cry.

Until I die he will not leave my side.]   40

NOTES

AUTHOR'S PROLOGUE (August 1952)
Written specially for *Collected Poems*, 1952. In a letter (10 September 1952) Thomas wrote: "I hope the Prologue *does* read as a prologue, and not as just another poem. I think—though I am too near it now to be any judge—that it *does* do what it sets out to do: addresses the readers, the 'strangers', with a flourish and fanfare, and makes clear, or tries to make clear, the position of one writer in a world 'at poor peace'." The Prologue ("this rumpus of shapes", l.37) dedicates the *Collected Poems* ("these seathumbed leaves", l.29).

The first and last lines rhyme, and so on inwards until the exact centre of the poem (lines 51 and 52) is a rhyming couplet.

ll.19–20 THE CITIES OF NINE / DAYS' NIGHT: the poet mixes two references to describe, mainly, London where he made his poetic and personal reputations: 'The City of Dreadful Night' and the proverbial phrase 'A nine days' wonder'.

l.33 DOGDAYED: 'Dog-days', named after the Dog-star, are the hottest days of the year, early July to middle August.

l.44 BELLOWING ARK: the sustained idea of Noah's Ark is an image of Thomas 'building' his poems as an act of survival.

l.56 DEER: the old sense of 'beasts', 'animals'.

l.57 BRYNS: Welsh for 'hills'.

BEING BUT MEN (May 1932)

OUT OF THE SIGHS (June–July 1932)
Compare Emily Dickinson's "After great pain, a formal feeling comes . . .", and Thomas Hardy's *In Tenebris*, part I.

Perhaps as a first entry into this poem the reader would do well to hold quite literally to the idea of disappointment in love; but it will also be seen that the poem registers a disaffection with life in general. Either way, the main emphasis is on a stoic realism about life's possibilities.

ll.1–4 The speaker has made a decision against holding a tragic view of life ("grief", "agony"). By giving in only to "sighs", he at least keeps himself open to a few cold comforts.

ll.7–9 The elliptical syntax can be opened out thus: 'There must, [God] be praised, [be] some certainty, if not [the certainty] of loving well, then [that of] not [loving well] . . .'

ll.10–11 cf. 'Cowards die many times before their deaths'.

ll.12–16 *General sense:* 'Even if someone eased the pain of the experience of parting, the ache continues because of the realization that regret which can be thus easily remedied is no regret at all.' ("Through no regret" here means 'because there is no regret'.)

ll.17–24 *General sense:* 'If mere regret after lost happiness could *completely* "ease the pain", or if 'vague' words and "lies" could do it, the speaker would willingly join in the hypocrisy of "hollow words".'

ll.25–28 *General sense:* 'If such remedies *were* completely adequate, it would suggest that man was as easily satisfied as a dog.'

ll.29–30 Man and his situation being more complicated than that, the speaker at least *recognizes* and *accepts* his dog's life!—its "crumbs" (meagre rewards), "barn" (poverty, imprisonment) and "halter" (tying-rope, noose).

OUT OF A WAR OF WITS (February 1933)
Around this time, Thomas and his friends used to meet regularly on Wednesday evenings at the poet's home in Swansea, for discussions and arguments which went on late into the night.

THEIR FACES SHONE UNDER SOME RADIANCE
(February 1933)

EARS IN THE TURRETS HEAR (July 1933)

Compare section V and VI of Yeats's *Meditations in Time of Civil War*, and Louis MacNeice's *Prognosis*.

"And living in your own private, four-walled world as exclusively as possible isn't escapism, I'm sure; it isn't the Ivory Tower, and, even if it were, you secluded in your Tower know and learn more of the world outside than the outside-man who is mixed up so personally and inextricably with the mud and the unlovely people." (Thomas in a letter to Vernon Watkins.) This poem is about the self-absorption of Thomas the man and the private nature of his poetic world. In short, it shows his fear and uncertainty in recognizing that "No man is an island unto himself".

THE HAND THAT SIGNED THE PAPER (August 1933)

Compare W. H. Auden's *Epitaph on a Tyrant*.

Thomas on the whole resisted the fashion of his generation for 'political' and 'socially conscious' poetry. This is the only poem in *Collected Poems* to be on an overtly political subject.

With one exception (line 4) the stanzas are regularly syllabic—11, 8, 11, 6.

l.2 SOVEREIGN: the proximity of "taxed" gives "sovereign" its monetary as well as its regal meaning.

l.4 FIVE KINGS: five fingers.

A KING: Christ may be suggested, as well as an ordinary, political king.

ll.5–6. The irony of "mighty" is driven home by references to the tyrant's "sloping shoulder" and his hand "cramped with chalk", which suggests both writer's cramp and arthritis.

ll.7–8. The two uses of "put an end to" have probably different meanings: 'a signature has as good as *accomplished* murder, which *put an end* to protest'.

l.15 The comparison with "heaven" and God has been led up to by the suggestion of the Old Testament in the previous stanza ("famine", "locusts").

THAT SANITY BE KEPT (September 1933)

Compare T. S. Eliot's *Morning at the Window*.

[pages 32–3]

BEFORE I KNOCKED (September 1933)

The speaker's consciousness predates, not only birth, but conception itself. Several hints in the poem make us think of that speaker as being Christ. But knowing how often Thomas fuses his own and everyman's identity with Christ, we can equally well take the primary speaker to be the poet, mythologized by analogies with Christ.

The poem has an unbroken syllabic count—lines of 9 and 8 syllables alternating throughout.

l.5 MNETHA: a name Thomas remembered from Blake's *Tiriel*. Its exotic sound seems, however, to be its only significance.

ll.23–24 The words "gallow crosses" and "brambles" suggest the crucifixion.

l.39 DEATH'S FEATHER: Cf. John Donne (*Devotions*): "There is scarce anything that hath not killed some body; a hair, a feather hath done it." But Thomas is equally likely to have been using the common expression 'You could have knocked me down with a feather'.

l.44 REMEMBER ME AND PITY HIM: Thomas is possibly suggesting that Christ was not, in the nature of things, able to fulfil Himself physically.

l.46 DOUBLECROSSED: *a* 'crossed twice' (God was both Father and Son in the Incarnation); *b* 'betrayed' (the idea that Christ may not have been the Son of God, as promised to Mary); *c* caused Mary to suffer twice—in the pain of birth and at Christ's later crucifixion.

It will be noticed, though, that Thomas writes "*my* mother's womb". The manuscript version, however, read "*his* mother's womb". If not a simple error, "my" may have been used to suggest *a* that *every* birth is an Incarnation, and *b* that Christ's birth doublecrosses or betrays every secular birth by establishing the inadequacy of a merely physical interpretation of life.

SONG ('Love me, not as the dreaming nurses . . .')
(September 1933)

[pages 34–5]

THE FORCE THAT THROUGH THE GREEN FUSE
DRIVES THE FLOWER (October 1933)

The identification of the world's elemental forces with those which govern the human body, so characteristic of Thomas's poetry, seems in itself clear enough. A greater difficulty would seem to lie in the repeated "And I am dumb to tell . . ." Thomas is possibly emphasizing the irony that, though physically man is one with the universe, he is separated from it by intellectual consciousness. In other words, the lament is not that he is dumb to tell, but that he can conceive of *telling* in the first place. In that sense, "dumb to tell" also means 'foolish to tell'.

l.2 BLASTS: not just 'blows on', but 'explodes' (see "fuse", l.1).

l.12 QUICKSAND: apart from the obvious meaning, there is possibly a reference to sand pouring quickly through an hour-glass, and a pun on 'quick' = living.

l.14 The "hanging man", being dead, is now genuinely one with the merely physical world to which the poet is dumb to tell.

l.15 HANGMAN'S LIME: the *quick*lime used to destroy the bodies of executed criminals buried in it.

l.16 THE FOUNTAIN HEAD: apart from the literal meaning, a metaphor for the womb from which time 'sucks' the newly born.

l.20 The line suggests that, under the pressure of Time, man has invented Eternity—ticking a heaven round the stars, just as a clock's hands, moving from hour to hour, ticks a perfect circle on the clock face.

l.22 Apart from the primary meaning, the "crooked worm" is possibly also the poet's finger moving on the "sheet" of paper on which the poem is written.

LIGHT BREAKS WHERE NO SUN SHINES
(November 1933)

Compare *When all my five and country senses see.*

"My own obscurity . . . is . . . based on a preconceived symbolism derived from the cosmic significance of the human anatomy" (Thomas in a letter). Here Thomas not so much compares as *identifies* the human body with the physical universe—an identification which elementalizes the body and personalizes the universe.

Only the penultimate line of the whole poem interrupts a regular syllabic count of 6, 10, 4, 10, 4, 10 in each stanza.

The following stanza-by-stanza paraphrase acts only as a guideline. It has had to avoid additional suggestions and alternative meanings at certain points.

I.   (ll.1–3) In the formed body, consciousness dawns like light, blood moves like a sea; (ll.4–6) two *simultaneous* meanings— at conception, light itself creates the flesh, and after death worms move through the earth which now *is* the flesh around the bones.

II. (ll.1–2) In the formed body, the sexual organs produce sperm, and destroy the sperm which is unused; (ll.3–5) before birth, the embryo uncurls like any fact of physical creation; (l.6) after death, when ordinary growth (pun on "wax") has ceased, the sexual organ is denuded like a candle of its wax.

III. (ll.1–3) In the formed body, consciousness dawns like light, blood moves like a sea; (ll.4–6) and because the universe is not different or separate (not "fenced" or "staked") rain is the same response to that process which 'divines' (discovers and makes holy) tears of grief behind a human smile.

IV. (ll.1–3) Sleep presages Death by darkening the eyes (a reminder also of the *limit*ations of ordinary eyesight); and as sight in daytime shows the body, *in*sight reveals the bone; (ll.4–6) after death, the flesh, like winter earth, is laid bare— but notions of warm and cold have ceased to matter; the thin thread which will produce spring growth is now literally fixed to the corpse's eyelid, corporate but unseen (pun on "film").

V.   After death, a *new* consciousness emerges, nothing to do with intellect, and in which abstract "thought" becomes physical sense, in which the mystery of growth, no longer an idea, is an actual growth in the skeleton's eyesockets, and in which blood vitalizes the plants responding to sunshine, life's source; (l.6) after this new organic consciousness, there is no other: "the dawn halts".

[pages 36–9]

A LETTER TO MY AUNT DISCUSSING THE CORRECT APPROACH TO MODERN POETRY (December 1933)

This was included in a letter to Pamela Hansford Johnson. In itself, of course, it is mere sport. But it serves as a useful reminder of Thomas's sense of humour and his mistrust of poetical 'fashions' or critical piety where poetry was concerned.

l.8 "David G." is David Gascoyne, the Surrealist poet mentioned in the Introduction to this volume.

THIS BREAD I BREAK (December 1933)

The poet's main emphasis is on the irony (pinpointed in the pun on "break") that the bread and wine which signify and give Christ's *life* in the Holy Communion are made from the *death* of nature. Characteristically, the poem resists man's tendency to abstract significance from an already significant (because vital) world. We remember Blake's assertion that "Everything that lives is Holy".

The manuscript bore the subtitle "Breakfast Before Execution" which makes us think of the Last Supper while still making a play on the word "break".

The syllabic structure of the poem is *un*broken, with lines of 8, 8, 4, 8, 8, syllables in each stanza.

l.2 A FOREIGN TREE: both the vine and the cross.

l.10 MAN BROKE THE SUN: with a play on the word Son (Christ).

ll.11–12 Because of the line-ending, we get the notion of sacrificial blood-letting ("this blood you let").

WHERE ONCE THE WATERS OF YOUR FACE
(March 1934)

Compare Wordsworth's *Ode: Intimations of Immortality*, and Thomas's *Poem in October* and *Fern Hill*.

In a letter roughly contemporary with this poem, Thomas wrote to a friend: "This new year has brought back to my mind the sense of magic that was lost—irretrievably I thought—so long ago." In the poem, Thomas uses the image of a rich and magical sea to denote a sense of wonder and optimism which he feels has passed, and the image of a dry sea bed to suggest the death of his childlike intuitions. As Wordsworth put it, "Shades of the prison-house begin to close/ Upon the growing Boy".

Each stanza has the same syllable count—8, 8, 6, 8, 8, 6.

l.1 WATERS OF YOUR FACE. cf. *Genesis* i. 2—"And the Spirit of God moved upon the face of the waters."

l.2 SPUN TO MY SCREWS: an abstract paraphrase might be 'Did my bidding'. The image also wittily suggests a boat's propellers. But it seems possible that a more private meaning also exists: in another poem, Thomas has the phrase "the screws that turn the voice", so he might be implying that the sea responded to his poetic voice. cf. "sang to my horn" in *Fern Hill*.

l.13 INVISIBLE: though the sea has withdrawn, the poet's imagination keeps it present as a potential.

ll.16–17 THE SHADES/ OF CHILDREN: a crucial phrase which suggests that the subject of the poem is the child's growth to maturity (cf. "the childless land" of *Fern Hill*). That part of the poet which is still childlike continues to yearn for the rich world of the imagination ("the dolphined sea", l.18).

ll.19–24 The final stanza affirms that the poet will strive to regain the child's vision. "Serpents" (l.23), however, acknowledges the presence of corruption inside all Edens.

I SEE THE BOYS OF SUMMER (April 1934)
Compare Thomas Hardy's *To an Unborn Pauper Child*.

The poet accuses the "boys of summer" of suppressing their natural sexuality. These "boys" can be taken to be the people he sees around him in his immediate community, and in stanzas three and four they are the unborn children who will become tomorrow's adolescents and adults. Most critics argue that Section II is spoken by the "boys of summer" themselves, in reply, and that Section III is a line-by-line dialogue between them and Thomas. The present editor believes that the whole poem is just as easily spoken by the poet on his own.

[pages 40–1]

Only line 47 breaks a syllable count of 11, 7, 10, 8, 8, 10 in each stanza.

The following stanza-by-stanza guide is designed to suggest the 'argument' of the poem, and therefore does not gloss all individual phrases and images. The main aspect the reader should note is the way in which the images constantly suggest the opposites, sexuality-frigidity, growth-decay, life-death. See also the discussion of the poem in the Introduction.

Stanza One: The boys of summer deny sexual fruition; they freeze, instead of using, their sexual potency. *Stanza Two:* They allow that which is sweet and productive to turn sour; masturbation takes the place of intercourse; they live off moral notions of "doubt and dark"; the female principle ("signal moon") means nothing to them. *Stanzas Three and Four:* The poet imagines the unborn children, and thinks they will grow ("stature") into "men of nothing" who will avoid sexual "heats"; their hearts already pump the warm pulse of conventional morality ("love and light"); but the natural pulse of blood is frozen, though seen as a potential by the poet.

Stanza Five: But, however the poet may despair, birth must happen—or *real* death takes over. *Stanza Six:* The poet now cynically acts as the spokesman of "the dark deniers", the society responsible for this frigid morality, summoning from the womb death instead of life, and scarecrows instead of vital flesh-and-blood. *Stanza Seven:* Speaking now as one of the "summer boys" already born, he attends at the birth of future generations, celebrated not with a bouquet, but with a cynically offered wreath. *Stanza Eight:* He claims that society as good as crucifies sexuality ("merry squires" = sexual organs); the sexual organ "dries and dies"; a kiss is allowed, but in the quarry of "no love". The last line, however, again points to the phallic "poles of promise" in the newly born.

Stanza Nine: A recapitulation. The final line suggests that their birth may change things. The image in that line is of the poles of two circles (womb and world) touching, as they merge into one at the moment of birth.

[pages 42-3]

ESPECIALLY WHEN THE OCTOBER WIND
(October 1934)

Two major themes come together in this poem. One of them, implicit in the imagery, is the theme of mutability and decay. The other, confirmed by similar statements in the letters and by an earlier, more prosaic version of the poem, is the theme of what we might call the tyranny of words. The poet feels that words keep replacing experience, that they come between him and the ordinary world.

Thomas seems to have worked to a basic count of 10 syllables per line.

Stanza One: The ordinary sensations of an October day, forecasting dissolution, makes his heart 'shudder' and respond in words, in poetry.

Stanza Two: The "tower of words" is both the poet's body and the house in which he works. The reality of the woman is for him literary ("wordy"), and the children in the park opposite cause him to make a pun on "rows" and fix on the star-pattern made by their arms and legs. He would like to communicate the reality of the "beeches" etc. at a level deeper than that of language; but the 'vowels', "voices" "notes" and "speeches" of words are his only tools.

Stanza Three: Things are communicated to him, not through words, but at the level of nervous ("neural") response. If only he could "tell" us what the meadow or the raven signifies in as wordless a way as the clock or grass "tells" him about the passing of time.

Stanza Four: But the poet gives in to the necessary limitations of words (though, within the brackets, he still emphasizes the wordless communications of nature). He now accepts his dependence on "heartless words"—heartless because they have been "drained" from the heart, and because they are not themselves alive. But having made these "heartless words" (having, that is, written this poem), his heart is now suitably word-less; and the final line asks us to listen, not to the words of this poem, but to the message of the "dark-vowelled birds".

I HAVE LONGED TO MOVE AWAY (December 1935)

Compare Philip Larkin's *Wants* and *Poetry of Departures*.

The speaker wishes to escape from social and religious conventions, which he considers bogus and hypocritical. But the thought worries him (lines 11–14) that convention, even if false, is nevertheless a form of security whereby the individual has at least company in facing the unknown, a kind of safety in numbers.

l.2 THE HISSING OF THE SPENT LIE suggests the serpent of *Genesis*, as well as the primary metaphor of a firework.

l.3 OLD TERRORS: the fears and superstitions on which society thrives.

l.7 SALUTES: apart from the military sense of discipline, the ordinary social courtesies, parodies of communication.

ll.8–9 One reason for wanting to escape is that conventional superstition ("ghosts in the air") is also dictating the attitudes of his poetry ("ghostly echoes on paper").

l.10 CALLS AND NOTES: apart from the military (and religious) idea of a trumpet sounding, there is the simpler notion of telephone-calls and visiting-cards (see line 17 below).

ll.15–18 The irony is that man, in any case, doesn't die from his superstitions and fears; whether he conventionally suffers from them or not, it is only death which kills him!

THE PARTING OF HAT FROM HAIR: the idea of hair standing on end (fright), and a repetition of the idea of social courtesy—a gentleman lifts his hat to ladies!

RECEIVER: telephone-receiver.

ll.19–20 *a* He 'would not mind' dying of these since, being bogus, they would make death itself unreal; but *b* neither 'would he choose to' let these obscure a more real sense of life and death.

SHOULD LANTERNS SHINE (December 1935)

Compare *Why east wind chills*.

The theme is the young man's determination to remain open to experience instead of seeking 'answers' or 'solutions' to the mystery of life. Something Keats once said is a good thing to bear in mind on approaching the poem—the need to allow "only a gradual ripening of the intellectual powers".

ll.1–8 The whole first stanza is a metaphor for man's tendency to probe and pry into the unknown. The image is of breaking into an Egyptian-style burial chamber, and finding the mummy disintegrating even as one looks at it.

l.2 OCTAGON: probably because the aperture of the lantern is octagonal, or because the tomb itself is.

ll.3–4 AND ANY BOY . . . FROM GRACE: any boy born of love, or intending love. There is a suggestion of necrophilia.

l.6 FALSE DAY: because *a* the lantern's light is artificial light, and *b* this is only a parody of the real Judgment Day.

ll.9–15 HEART . . . HEAD . . . PULSE: Three 'philosophies of life' which the young man has had urged upon him. He mistrusts each one in isolation. "like head" (l.10) refers back to the first stanza, which was an image of the workings of pure reason.

ll.11–14 cf. for interest, Andrew Marvell's *To His Coy Mistress*:
> Rather at once our Time devour,
> Than languish in his slow-chapt pow'r.
> . . . .
> Thus, though we cannot make our Sun
> Stand still, yet we will make him run.

l.17 SOME CHANGE: either change as the result of the advice ("telling"), or change in the advice itself.

ll.18–19 The "ball" is an image of a question, to which no answer has "yet reached the ground". Time and experience have to be lived through before they become, in themselves, the answer. The image is one of many memories in the poetry of Cwmdonkin Park, directly in front of Thomas's childhood home in Swansea.

INCARNATE DEVIL (January 1936)
Like Blake, Thomas here sees the separation of good and evil as a case of abstract distinctions, superimposed upon man's deeper

instincts. Compare Blake in *The Marriage of Heaven and Hell*: "Without contraries is no progression. Attraction and Repulsion, Reason and Energy, Love and Hate, are necessary to Human existence. From these contraries spring what the religious call Good & Evil. Good is the passive that obeys Reason. Evil is the active springing from Energy."

The following is a working paraphrase, which by no means follows through every suggestion made by the poem's images:

I The Biblical Eden, seen in a way which makes God guilty of setting an arbitrary trap for man. Through the serpent (which the poet would rather see as the vitality which "stung awake" the "circle" of the apple, the garden, or the world itself), God gave the *appearance* of evil ("shapes of sin") to the "forked" Tree of Knowledge. He prohibited ("forked out") and set apart ("forked out") the apple which "bearded" God Himself had created. In this event, God acted the part of unconcerned "fiddling" Nero and deceitful ("fiddling") boss—having in the first place arranged it to exercise His own power of pardon, and minimizing ('playing down') His own need for pardon in such trickery.

II Scholars tell me that in pagan times, when men were strangers to the idea of God-controlled seas or the idea that God created the moon by hand, the pagan deities *united* good and evil. The moon, itself a deity, was black *and* white in its significance for man, not the one-sided white ("half holy", 'half whole') of Christian thought.

III In our own non-mythological Eden (in the womb or in childhood), we had an intuitive ("secret") belief in a force ("guardian". Innocence?) which would keep that paradise from the Fall of Experience. But the notion of a burning Hell, or the idea that things are either good *or* bad ("the cloven myth"), or that the only heaven comes through the death of Christ ('midnight of the Son') which occurred in darkness ("midnight of the sun")—these were the "fiddled" tunes and "fiddled" tricks of a Christian God, seen now as the serpent itself.

[pages 45–6]

WHY EAST WIND CHILLS (January 1936)

Compare Robert Frost's *Neither Out Far Nor In Deep* and his *The Most Of It*, Robert Graves's *Warning to Children* and Thomas's *Should lanterns shine* and *This Side of the Truth*.

The theme is man's necessary ignorance of any final answers in the face of a mysterious universe.

l.1 The basic futility of the questions makes fun of man's tendency to seek intellectual explanations of natural mysteries.

l.2 WINDWELL: the source of the winds, something like Aeolus's cave of winds in classical mythology.

l.10 COMETH: the archaic form makes the question appear both quaint and timeless.

> JACK FROST suggests on the one hand innocent winter magic and, on the other, Death.

l.11 The "comet" represents an answer to a metaphysical question. The image is borrowed from John Donne's *Song* "Go, and catch a falling star . . .".

> FISTS: clenched hands suggest defiance and frustration where a more relaxed receptivity should be.

ll.16–20 "All things are known" is ironically intended. Astrology ("the stars' advice") gives some people a false confidence that they are in league with the mysterious order of things. But only the end of the world will show how much the stars themselves are ignorant of!

l.19 TOWERS: originally Thomas had written "houses", suggesting that he means the various stations of the Zodiac.

l.21 CONTENT: both noun (*content*ment) and adverb (*content*edly).

HERE IN THIS SPRING (January 1936)

In nature, impressions of beauty and growth coexist with signs of death.

ll.1–4 Mixed in with conventional associations ("spring", "*ornamental* winter") are darker indications of extinction and suffering—the stars float in a "void", and line 3 reminds us of the storm in *King Lear*. Even summer, the height of life and growth, is a death—of spring.

l.3 Puns on "down" (= feathers = snow) and "pelts" (= animal skins) give a secondary meaning to the line—'down-like snow clothes the naked weather'.

ll.7–8 The implication is that while, on the one hand, autumn fruitfulness makes us think only of "three seasons" (spring, summer and autumn itself), autumn's decay reminds us that it takes winter to complete the full cycle of four.

l.9 I SHOULD TELL: 'I would think it' summer if I looked only at the trees.

l.12 I SHOULD LEARN: 'I would expect' spring if I listened only to the cuckoo which heralds it.

l.14 BETTER: 'more truthfully', because the worm also tells us that summer will pass.

l.16 WHAT SHALL IT TELL ME: 'What exactly is the significance of the message that the world wears away, and what the responsibilities that go along with knowing it?'

AND DEATH SHALL HAVE NO DOMINION
(February 1936)

Compare Donne's Holy Sonnet "Death be not proud . . .", Shelley's *Adonais*, stanzas 39–44, and Thomas's *A Refusal to Mourn the Death, by Fire, of a Child in London*.

l.1 This repeated line is based on a clause in St Paul's Epistle to the Romans (vi. 9): "Christ being raised from the dead dieth no more; death hath no more dominion over him." And lines 7 and 11–12 remind us of *Revelation* (xx. 13): "And the sea gave up the dead which were in it." But Thomas's poem is more pantheistic than Christian. What it affirms is the indissolubility of the general fact and principle of Life, not any promise of individual Christian resurrection.

l.3 A juggled reference to the man in the moon and the west wind.

l.12 WINDILY: mainly 'in vain'; but a slang meaning would also seem appropriate—'in a state of fright'. The word has been brought to mind by "windings" in the previous line.

ll.13–18 These lines suggest the death of martyrs (St Catherine was tortured and killed on a spiked wheel). Even if their faith gives way, the defeat of an ideology is never the end of Life itself.

UNICORN EVILS: the phrase suggests both the brutalities of torture and the rending spiritual pains involved in a loss of faith.

ll.19–23 Natural phenomena—the cry of gulls, the sound of the sea, a flower—in a sense owe their existence to the human perception which recognizes and appreciates them. If one judges merely from the viewpoint of an individual, the natural world would appear to die when the individual dies. Individuality dies, but general cosmic life continues.

l.25 cf. the euphemism 'Pushing up daisies'. "Hammer" was probably suggested by "nails" in the previous line.

l.26 BREAK: break open (with the flowers).

THE SPIRE CRANES (November 1937)
Compare Thomas's *Once it was the colour of saying* and *On no work of words.*
The spire is an image of the poet. The stone birds carved in the masonry stand for those poems which, because they are either too artificially made or too private in their meaning, fail to escape into communication with the outside world. In contrast, the chimes and the real living birds suggest a more vital and communicating kind of poetry, because they escape from the poet-spire.

Line 6 is the only exception to a syllabic count of 12 in each line.

ll.2–3 THE FEATHERY/ CARVED BIRDS: the carved birds are covered with the moulted feathers of the real birds.

l.4 THE SPILT SKY: the sea.

l.6 THAT PRIEST, WATER: cf. Keats's 'Bright star' sonnet—"waters at their priestlike task/ Of pure ablution round earth's human shores."

ll.7–8 SILVER LOCK/ AND MOUTH suggest the singing voice.

ll.9–11 The more artificial, private poems pose a problem of choice for the poet. Should he stop writing them? As they stand, they communicate only backwards to the poet himself.

[pages 48–9]

They do not get soiled and tested in the real world (like the Prodigal Son) before returning.

O MAKE ME A MASK (November 1937)

Compare Thomas's *I have longed to move away, Ears in the turrets hear,* and *To Others than You.*

The man, and possibly the poet, seeks defence of inner privacy against the blunt examination of outsiders or critics.

Except for line 7, all the lines have 13 syllables.

l.2 ENAMELLED EYES . . . SPECTACLED CLAWS: the adjectives have been transferred.

l.3 Behind a face of innocence, he seeks to hide the harrowing effects of time and experience.

l.4 BARE ENEMIES: "bare" because they would be disarmed by his pretence.

l.10 BELLADONNA: Deadly Nightshade. The literal meaning (Beautiful Lady) contrasts with the pretended modesty of "widower grief".

ll.10–12 From behind his own pretence, he will more easily detect the pretence of others. The "curve of the nude mouth" and "the laugh up the sleeve" belong to the speaker and his enemies alike.

AFTER THE FUNERAL (IN MEMORY OF ANN JONES) (Spring 1938)

Compare Hopkins's *Felix Randall,* and the first story in Thomas's *Portrait of the Artist as a Young Dog.*

Ann Jones was the poet's maternal aunt who lived at Fern Hill, where Thomas spent many schoolboy holidays. After the hypocrisy of the mourners (ll.1–5) and the emotional poverty of the poet's first response to Ann's death (ll.7–8), Thomas offers an exaggerated 'Bardic' eulogy which is made to contrast with the old woman's simplicity (ll. 16–20) and with the pious finality of her death (ll. 31–35). A sustained theme is the inadequacy of language to keep human reality alive; but the poem's poignancy lies nevertheless in that attempt.

l.5 SPITTLED EYES: the mourner's eyes show only a pretence at grief.

ll.6–8 In the presence (presumably) of the open coffin in the farm parlour early on the morning of the funeral, the young boy was at the time incapable of adequate emotion, shedding "dry leaves" instead of tears; but a promise was made that he would produce the "dry leaves" of a future poem.

l.25 A BROWN CHAPEL: the natural chapel of "the ferned and foxy woods".

l.27 THIS SKYWARD STATUE: the exaggerated description of Ann is compared to a monumental statue on a gravestone.

l.37 GESTURE AND PSALM: as nouns, the "gesture" made by Ann's imagined statue and the "psalm" of the poem's praise; as also verbs, the two words are in apposition to "storm" in the next line.

ll.36–40 The sense of these last five lines is a hope that the exaggerated description of Ann and the poem itself will keep alive the poet's emotional relationship to the old woman, and return a less artificial life to the home and community she has left.

WHEN ALL MY FIVE AND COUNTRY SENSES SEE
(August 1938)

The speaker of this sonnet is an unborn human being. He looks forward to two distinct stages after birth: *a* ll.1–12, the stage of an ordinary life-span and *b* ll.13–14, the stage after death. Stage *a* is when our understanding is informed by (and restricted to) our physical senses. Stage *b* is the different situation after death when there is a kind of organic, cosmic consciousness—undivided, and no longer open to disappointment. Only line 13 breaks a regular syllabic count of 10 syllables per line.

ll.1–10 Four senses (touch, hearing, taste, smell) are described as having the power of 'seeing', which is of course the fifth sense. What they will 'see' in life is how love is all the time being reduced, delayed, driven out and ruined.

l.1 COUNTRY: 'physical', also suggesting that each sense is a separate "country" (cf. "love's countries", l.12).

ll.3–4 The 'halfmoons' on the fingernails are compared also to the
"husk of young stars". Like Zodiacal signs on a human hand,
they forecast the death and denial of "love".

l.8 LASHED TO SYLLABLES: 'whipped to pieces' and/or 'tied
(limited) to words'. The tongue will be powerless to remedy
the injury done to love.

ll.9, 10 HER: love's.

l.14 After death, the heart will continue a "sensual", sub-intellec-
tual consciousness as part of the organic world itself.

THE TOMBSTONE TOLD WHEN SHE DIED
(September 1938)

Thomas, in a letter, described this poem as "Hardy-like",
referring presumably to its anecdotal quality. From several time-
angles, the poem centres on the story of a girl who died before the
sexual fulfilment of her marriage-night.

l.2 HER TWO SURNAMES: her maiden and her married surnames.

ll.6–9 Her marriage occurred before the poet was conceived. But
the embryo's pre-natal experience of life and death was as
good as being a *fore*casting vision of this girl's individual dead
body.

ll.11–20 (Second Stanza). After coming across her grave, the poet
hears gossip of how she had died. Dying itself was like the
sexual fulfilment which was in actuality denied her (ll.17–20).

l.11 A STRANGER: her husband—whom Death prevented her
'knowing' sexually.

ll.13–15. This happened (the poet repeats) before the poet's
pre-natal vision of the girl's dead body, before the rain
running through her heart 'spoke' (l.8) her death to the
embryo in the womb ("the room of a secret child").

l.21 I WHO SAW is the embryo who experienced her death like a film
thrown on the "mortal wall" of the womb.

l.24 HEARD refers to the poet's experience while actually standing
by her grave. Now, as if speaking through the "stone bird"
carved on her tombstone, the girl describes her own death.

ll.29–30 These two final lines concentrate two ideas: the sexual fulfilment of death; and the *imagined* birth of a son.

ON NO WORK OF WORDS (September 1938)

Compare Milton's sonnet "When I consider how my light is spent", Keats's sonnet "When I have fears that I may cease to be", and Hopkins's sonnet *To R[obert] B[ridges]*.

To partake of the created world involves, for the artist, the responsibility of reproducing its creativity in return. From the word "rich" (l.2) springs a sustained series of financial imagery.

l.1 The words suggest being on the dole.

l.3 TAKE TO TASK: reprimand; but also, literally, 'bring to the job' which needs doing.

l.4 HUNGRILY: God sent down manna to feed the hungry Israelites (*Exodus* xvi), some of whom refused the gift so that the manna "bred worms and stank". The position of "hungrily" here suggests that God himself is hungry for a response.

l.5 cf. George Herbert's images for *Prayer*: "reversed thunder", "exalted manna".

l.6 Unused, the poet's 'gift' for words returns as an insult ("bangs back"), its powers of revelation wasted ("blind").

l.7 TO LIFT TO LEAVE: to accept and then abandon is a form of stealing ('lifting').

TREASURES OF MAN: either the wonders of the created world, or the poems of other poets (?)

ll.8–9 Death will, like a cashier, balance all used opportunities against those left unused, in a final judgment.

l.10 OGRE: Death.

TWICE: Death takes, not only the poet's body, but also that body of poetry he failed to produce.

ll.11–12 In a sense, the world exists only as we, in responding to it, are constantly recreating it ("this world . . . is each man's work", l.12). Thus if the poet merely exhausts it selfishly ("burn", l.12), it dwindles (the forest becomes the nut again). If, however, he 'under*takes*' to respond creatively ("return", l.12), the creation of the world will be reproduced in each poem (the nut will be seen to produce the woods).

THE NUT OF THE SEAS: all life is thought to have originated in the sea.

WHICH IS EACH MAN'S WORK: with "to return" as its subject, this clause reads 'which is each man's duty'; with "world" as its subject, it reads 'which is each man's creation'.

TWENTY-FOUR YEARS (October 1938)

Written a few days before the poet's twenty-fourth birthday. Compare Milton's sonnet on *his* twenty-fourth birthday, "How soon hath Time, the subtle thief of youth".

l.2 IN LABOUR: with difficulty; but also in the act of giving birth. The line, one supposes, is mainly relevant because of its ominous tone, reminiscent of an 'Aside' in a Jacobean tragedy.

l.3 NATURAL DOORWAY: the entrance of the womb, where life's "journey" starts.

l.4 SHROUD: both the winding-sheet in which the dead body will be finally dressed, and the flesh of the body itself.

ll.6–8 Life is seen as keeping a date with death ("dressed . . . strut . . . money . . . direction . . . town").

l.6 DIE: also a pun on the Elizabethan sense of sexual fulfilment.

l.8 ELEMENTARY: death seen as a primary, basic fact. The word also suggests 'elemental'.

l.9 The speaker is open-minded as to how long Time is, or whether Eternity exists. This last line transforms the melodrama of the poem into a note of resignation, with a subtle suggestion of value ("advance") and into the irony of a poem about death ending with the verb 'to be'—"as long as forever *is*"!

ONCE IT WAS THE COLOUR OF SAYING (December 1938)

Compare Yeats's *A Coat, The Circus Animals' Desertion,* and Robert Graves's *The Cool Web*.

A kind of interim report on the poet's own career. Thomas feels that hitherto the glamour of words has counted more with him than the human experience which poetry ought to be exploring.

l.1 COLOUR OF SAYING: the rhetorical and aesthetic sound and shape of words, as opposed to what they actually mean.

l.2 SOAKED: the first of several hints that his love for mere language tended to drown and wash away the reality of his subjects ("soaked . . . capsized . . . seaslides . . . drowned"). The "table" is his writing-table.

UGLIER SIDE OF A HILL: Thomas's childhood home at Cwmdonkin Drive, Swansea was on a very steep suburban hill ("uglier" than the country the other side).

l.3 CAPSIZED: the steep road made the field opposite the house appear as if on the wrong level. The word also suggests 'the size of a cap'.

ll.5–6 The glamorous language had drowned the people and other realities in the poems. Now they will resurrect themselves ("arise"), herald a new dawn in the poet's career ("cockcrow"), and "kill" the old poet.

l.7 MITCHING: slang-word common in Wales = 'playing truant'.

l.8 CUCKOO: mad, silly.

ll.10–11 "Shade", a word denoting darkness, had been capable of several "shades" (associations) of meaning—and therefore something spectacular and *colour*ful ("a lamp of lightning").

l.12 Now his poetry *a* shall be an "undoing" of his old manner (cf. "I must undo", l.5); *b* shall savour less of the poet himself and more of outside reality; *c* may even be the *final* end of him as a poet if his new manner is not successful.

l.13 The effect of this last line is to contrast the hard reality ("stone") of the new poetry with the verbal *gentle*ness and *charm* (ll.5–6) of the earlier style; and to contrast a new deliberateness ("wind off like a reel") with the old style's hectic "sea*slides* of saying" (l.5). Though "reel" may suggest a cinema camera, it is more likely that of a fishing rod.

'IF MY HEAD HURT A HAIR'S FOOT' (March 1939)
Compare Louis MacNeice's *Prayer Before Birth*, and Sylvia Plath's *Nick and the Candlestick*.
Thomas's first child, Llewelyn, was born in January 1939. *Stanzas*

One–Three are spoken by an unborn child; *stanzas Four–Six* are the mother's reply to the child's fears of causing her pain in birth.

l.4 WORM OF THE ROPES: the umbilical cord; Thomas made "ropes" plural to suggest its coiled appearance, and also to introduce several images of the boxing-ring.

l.5 BULLY ILL LOVE: the verb is "bully ill".
   CLOUTED: in the sense of both 'beaten' and 'cloths'.

l.9 THE GHOST WITH A HAMMER, AIR: Thomas probably remembered that Jimmy Wilde, the Welsh boxing hero, was nicknamed 'The ghost with a hammer in his hand'.

l.12 THE MAKING HOUSE: the womb.

l.16–17 The mother would not change this birth for the presumably gentler birth of Christ or the slow process which brings mother-of-pearl (nacre) into being.

l.20 One allusion is to the 'breaking of the waters' of the womb, technically the first stage of birth.

l.30 "Prodigies" here suggests that *all* children are marvels. This one birth ("beginning"), though painful ("suffers"), is "endless" and "open" because it will lead to countless others.

TO OTHERS THAN YOU (May 1939)

Compare Thomas's *O make me a mask.*

The poet's accusation is that friendship has been used as a cover to lay bare his inner privacy. The main syntax runs: "You . . . Whom now I conjure to stand as thief . . . Were once such a creature . . . (That) I never thought to utter or think . . . That . . . My friends were enemies on stilts . . ."

l.1 BY ENEMY: by calling you an enemy.

l.17 DISPLACED A TRUTH: by speaking a lie.

PAPER AND STICKS (Autumn 1939)

Thomas included this poem in his fourth volume of poetry, *Deaths and Entrances* (1946), but omitted it from his *Collected Poems* (1952) at the proof stage.

[pages 56–7]

WHEN I WOKE (Autumn 1939)

Morning sounds in Laugharne wake Thomas from his private night-mares and to his work as a poet. But a new 'voice' heralds a different nightmare—the outbreak of the Second World War—which will end the ordinary world as he knows it.

ll.3–7 The images are from the world of his own nightmares. "Dispelled" (l.6) = not only 'dispersed' but 'broke the spell of'.

ll.8–15 An ordinary workman, concerned only with the physical, 'cuts the morning off' from the world of nightmare, as if he were killing the "last snake" of the poet's dream-world or the "wand or subtle bough" which would lead him back into nightmare.

ll.16–21 The poet sees himself as God (because he creates a world in his poetry), capable of miracle (walking on the water), and marking the "fall" of the "sparrow" and of the "death-stagged scatter-breath mammoth".

l.25 ERECTED AIR: either because the announcement of war comes over the radio, or because the clocks and bells of l.28 are on 'erected' towers.

ll.29–30 The two final images of "white sheet" and "coins on my eyelids" suggest death. There are second meanings to both "islands" ('eye-lands') and "shells" (bombs).

THERE WAS A SAVIOUR (February 1940)

The poem emphasizes man's *individual* responsibility for love and compassion. In the past, Christianity has been a kind of comforting other-worldly retreat from that responsibility. Now, in a less religious age, and in the first winter of the Second World War, human tragedy is brought home to each individual conscience. In this direct confrontation with those who have perverted Christ's teaching, Thomas gains an added irony by using the stanza-form of Milton's *On the Morning of Christ's Nativity*.

Stanza One describes those first Christians who thus blinded themselves to outside reality. *Stanza Two* is spoken by those

Christians themselves, confessing their fault. *Stanza Three* is addressed by the poet to those Christians, repeating the accusation. *Stanzas Four and Five* are spoken by the poet and one of those nominal Christians, the poet thereby confessing his own guilt in the matter.

l.4 CHILDREN: either the earliest Christian believers or literally children (perhaps in Sunday School?).

l.8 JAILS AND STUDIES: Christianity seen as a teaching and a discipline to which men blindly confine themselves. The word "keyless", however, suggests that the fault lies with Christians, not with Christ. Christ's actual teaching involved, not easy safety, but '*cruel* truth' (l.3), "safe *unrest*" (l.11), "*murdering* breath" (l.14) etc.

l.10 LOST WILDERNESS: the 'safety' of blind Christianity was not a paradise but a "wilderness", divorced from the actual world of men.

ll.22–23 Their emotion was directed to heaven, not to earth.

l.24 Now the responsibility falls directly on individuals.

l.25 BLACKED: morally guilty; caught in the darkness of individual responsibility; but also in the darkness of a wartime black-out.

l.30 NEAR AND FIRE NEIGHBOUR: "fire" evokes the blitz; but there is also a play on 'near and far'.

l.32 LITTLE KNOWN FALL: the death of any ordinary person, as opposed to the more 'famous' fall of Adam or the death of Christ.

ll.37–38 The dust of dead strangers enters through doors previously closed to them.

ll.39–40 The love which had previously been isolated inside each individual. The "rocks" it will 'break' could be the rock of cruelty, the rock guarding Christ's tomb, and even the rock of the church itself.

ON THE MARRIAGE OF A VIRGIN (July 1941)
A working paraphrase of *Stanza One*: When the girl was a virgin, each new morning's sun discovered ("surprised") yesterday's sun

asleep (like another guilty lover) on the iris of her now open eye—
as if having slept with her. And each new sun was almost like a son
born from the previous night's union, leaping "up the sky out of
her thighs". Though literally unmarried ("alone"), the virginity
which woke up each day in such "a multitude of loves" was, there-
fore, a "miraculous" one, having produced something like Mary's
immaculate conception of Christ, and as old as Christ himself. But,
as the *multiplication* of the loaves and fishes implies, miracles are
not unproductive; each miracle is "unending" in what it produces,
because each survives the "moment" in which it took place. Thus
the "footprints" which Christ made while walking on the waters
of Galilee were as productive as a whole "navy of doves"—those
birds sacred to Venus and profane love.

l.14 This final line suggests that her new relationship with a single
husband is both narrower ("jealous") *and* greater ("un-
rivalled").

THE HUNCHBACK IN THE PARK (July 1941)
Compare W. H. Auden's "It was Easter as I walked in the public
gardens".

This is not in the ordinary sense fiction: the hunchback, the warning
bell, the chained cup etc. were for the poet actual memories of
Cwmdonkin Park, Swansea. The relationship of the hunchback to
the "figure without fault" (l.32) which he creates is perhaps a
suggestion of that between the mortal poet and the created poem;
so that Thomas here is, all at once, the narrating poet, one of the
tormenting boys, and the hunchback himself.

l.4 LOCK: literally a lock on the park gate, and metaphorically an
image of the gate itself as a canal 'lock' allowing entrance and
exit.

l.5 The child imagined that the park existed only when he was
there. Cf. *Fern Hill*, ll.23–29.

l.31 MADE: possibly the figure is to be thought of as being traced
in the dust; but more likely as a daydream of the hunch-
back's.

AMONG THOSE KILLED IN THE DAWN RAID WAS A MAN AGED A HUNDRED (August 1941)

Compare Thomas's *A Refusal to Mourn the Death, by Fire, of a Child in London*.

Characteristically, this sonnet refuses to let the *natural* triumph of the old man's death be obscured by piety, officialdom or propaganda.

l.2 HE DIED: by using this phrase instead of 'was killed', Thomas emphasizes a natural process instead of a political catastrophe. A man aged a hundred is presumably already near death.

l.3 THE LOCKS: in line 11 the man's body is described as a "cage". The "locks" which keep in his life were already 'yawning loose' before the bomb blast "blew them wide".

l.4 LOVED: play on 'lived'.

l.6 HE STOPPED A SUN: "sun" = bomb. But also literally: for him the sun went out.

ll.10–14 Presumably the ambulance is called "heavenly" because it would be a Red Cross vehicle, collecting the dead for a Christian burial. It is a "common cart" because it collects *all* the dead. The uniqueness of this centenarian victim should give him the right to lie "where he loved". Instead of an ordinary Christian resurrection, the poet stresses that the literal morning is not stopped but quickened by the man's death; and implies that every one of his hundred years will be resurrected by the next hundred births ("storks") in this very place.

CEREMONY AFTER A FIRE RAID (May 1944)

"It really is a Ceremony, and the third part of the poem is the music at the end" (Thomas, in a letter).

l.4 AMONG makes the singular "street" stand for *all* streets, as the poet stands for all "grievers".

l.8 DUG: strictly a verb, but also a noun in apposition to "breast".

ll.14–15 The falling "star" of the incendiary bomb (unlike the star which signalled Christ's birth?) has ended the "centuries" of human lives which would have come from this one child.

l.21 A GREAT FLOOD: perhaps of the words in this tumultuous poem, metaphorically resuscitating the blood-flow of the dead child.

l.28 BEYOND COCKCROW: beyond actual resurrection.

l.29 THE FLYING SEA: an image for the resurgence of Life.

l.31 LOVE: the creative principle of Life—the first, last, and only fact. The word "spoken" reminds us that "God *said*, Let there be light" and that "In the beginning was the *Word*".

ll.31–32 The poet's only lament at this stage is for the unborn "sons" of the dead child.

ll.33–46 All sacrificed victims are one; this child represents them all; its skeleton is the gravestone (l.44) of all sacrificed innocence.

ll.51–56 The "one child" is mainly Christ who both conquered the serpent and was Himself the "fruit" and 'son' of what the serpent did to Eve.

ll.58–60 Thomas leaves Section II on a note of desolation (as if creation, in this event, had returned to chaos and wilderness), but does so in order to contrast and set off the affirmation of the final section which follows.

ll.61–77 The language evokes a literal landscape of burning cathedrals and churches. The surging image of the sea suggests, however, that what will survive is not a Christian consolation as such, but the irresistible, sexual force of life. The "infant-bearing sea" is endless; the fact of birth ("genesis"), once established, is final and "ultimate".

LAST NIGHT I DIVED MY BEGGAR ARM and POEM ('Your breath was shed . . .') (June 1944)

POEM IN OCTOBER (August 1944)
Compare Henry Vaughan's *Regeneration*.
One of the poet's many birthday poems. The location is Laugharne in Carmarthenshire, viewed (from stanza three onwards) from Sir John's Hill.
Only lines 55 and 56 break the regular syllabic count of 9, 12, 9, 3, 5, 12, 12, 5, 3, 9 in each stanza.
l.2 WOKE: the subject of "woke" is "the morning" (l.5).

l.8 MYSELF: the object of "beckon(ing)" (l.5).

l.40 THE WEATHER TURNED AROUND: stanzas three and four have depicted a freak phenomenon—bright sunshine on the hill, but mist and rain below. Then in line 40 Thomas records an even greater phenomenon—the ability of memory (of childhood) to transform and transcend merely external weather. The difference is drawn between *external* delight ("marvel", l.38) and *inward* vision ("And I saw . . . so clearly", l.46), between fancy ("tall tales", l.36) and real imagination.

l.42 THE OTHER AIR: that of vision and memory.

l.50 GREEN CHAPELS: woods.

l.51 TWICE TOLD: first lived through, and later remembered. There is the common pun on "told" = counted.

HOLY SPRING (November 1944)

Waking from "a bed of love" to a world violently at war, the poet is forced to question in what way his work can remain affirmative and celebratory.

l.3 THAT IMMORTAL HOSPITAL: the "bed of love".

l.4 COUNTED BODY: because its days are numbered.

ll.8–9 The poet's involvement is not with the war's rights and wrongs, but with the fact that life ("light") is in any case borrowed time.

l.12 Presumably the sun makes him feel lonely because its confident reappearance contrasts with the poet's own feelings. "Holy maker" = poet.

l.18 PRODIGAL: because the sun has been away, wasting his beams elsewhere.

l.19 The sun symbolizes the Life principle. It will father new lives, almost as a revenge for the loss of those infants killed in the London raids.

ll.20–24 But the poet chooses instead to celebrate the anarchy and "upheaval", because (to paraphrase line 21) 'Since that turmoil is still with us, the only real certainty for the poet lies in standing alone and producing song from the midst of uncertainty'. "Toppling house" suggests the changing Zodiac.

THE CONVERSATION OF PRAYER (March 1945)

Compare Hardy's *On One Who Lived and Died Where He Was Born.*

The curious music of this poem is produced by the mixture of end-rhymes with carefully placed internal rhymes (e.g. stanza one: prayers-stairs-tears, said-bed-dead, love-move, room-whom). The way in which rhymes cross in the middle of lines is a structural reflection of the main theme—the crossing of two individual prayers.

l.1 CONVERSATION: a second meaning wittily implied is that of 'change': the situation of the man and the boy in the last stanza is the 'converse' of what it is in the first. A similar pun is made on the word "Turns" in line six.

A REFUSAL TO MOURN THE DEATH, BY FIRE, OF A CHILD IN LONDON (March 1945)

Compare Wordsworth's "A slumber did my spirit seal" and William Soutar's *The Children* (included in the 'Everyman's Library' *Poems of Our Time*).

Unlike its negative title, the poem's tone is affirmative and positive in its evocation of the child's return into cosmic life. What it 'refuses' to do is fall into pious lament or propaganda.

ll.1–4 The subject of "tells" is "darkness". As the original darkness out of which life was created, it is described as 'making mankind', 'fathering bird, beast and flower', and 'humbling all'. The poem implies that the darkness will never again become a void.

ll.4–6 Note how these lines balance the negatives with positives: "*Tells* with *silence*", "the *last* light *breaking*", "the *still* hour . . . of the sea *tumbling* in harness".

ll.8–9 "Zion" and "synagogue" make sacred the world of nature to which human life, in death, returns.

l.11 SALT SEED: tears.

l.12 SACKCLOTH (and ashes) are Old Testament signs of mourning.

l.14 MURDER: obscure, or make a travesty of.

l.15 THE MANKIND OF HER GOING: the 'naturalness' of her death (cf. Chaucer, "for no man can undo the law of kind [nature]"). In Shakespeare, the masculine word "mankind", when applied to a female, connotes cruelty ("the *man*kind of *her* going").

l.16 STATIONS OF THE BREATH: a play on 'stations of the cross'.

l.19 THE FIRST DEAD: the simplest meaning seems as strong as any other, i.e. the first mortals who ever died.

l.20 ROBED IN THE LONG FRIENDS: mixed with the "grains" and "veins" of others 'long' since dead. "Friends" suggests the kinship in death which life's hostilities denied.

l.21 THE DARK VEINS OF HER MOTHER: "mother" = *a* the girl's actual mother, *b* London (cf. "London's daughter", l.19), and *c* mother-earth. The last sense gives "veins" another meaning.

l.24 Though provocatively ambiguous, this last line promises, not resurrection, but continuing organic life.

THIS SIDE OF THE TRUTH (FOR LLEWELYN)
(March 1945)

Compare Yeats's *A Prayer for my Son*, Auden's *Lullaby* ("Lay your sleeping head, my love . . ."), and Thomas's *In country sleep*.

Llewelyn was the poet's son, his first child, aged six when the poem was written. The poem claims that, however man himself may distinguish between Good and Bad, he does so in a completely neutral universe. Outside man, there is neither approval nor disapproval.

l.1 THIS SIDE OF THE TRUTH: this side of death, or this side of maturity.

l.13 GOOD AND BAD: this phrase is the subject of the next three main verbs ("Blow away", "Go crying", "Fly").

ll.23–28 In a completely physical world, death shows that Good and Bad have only an *imagined* reality. Like the "stars' blood", the "sun's tears", and the "moon's seed [sperm]", they are the result of man's tendency to anthropomorphize the 'elemental' universe.

[pages 70–2]

l.29 WICKED WISH: the "wish" is the basic impulse towards creativity; only man's self-consciousness can make it appear "wicked".

l.36 LOVE: the word "love", in this context, draws all its meaning from its adjective, "unjudging".

A WINTER'S TALE (March 1945)

As a phrase, "a winter's tale" traditionally refers to a story told, not for its significance, but for the more trivial aim of whiling away a winter evening. Though Thomas's poem owes nothing important to Shakespeare's *The Winter's Tale*, both titles heighten (by first denying) the tragic proportions of the stories they introduce. Such titles also warn us that the tales will not be completely realistic ones.

It seems clear that the "she-bird" embodies mainly the regenerative power of sexual love, delivering the man from the winter world of loneliness, old age, and the seasons. To what degree she also symbolizes Death, each reader must decide.

The poem's stanzas are apportioned as follows: *Stanzas 1–2* (Present tense) the in-coming twilight carries with it a story associated with the described landscape. *Stanzas 3–11* (Past tense) the tale itself starts being told. *Stanzas 12–13* (Present tense) an address to the reader, saying that all previous life seems reborn in the landscape. *Stanza 14* (Past tense) one stanza developing the tale itself: the "she-bird" appears. *Stanzas 15–16* (Present tense) another address to the reader, like stanzas twelve–thirteen. *Stanzas 17–22* (Past tense) the tale itself continued: the man follows the "she-bird". *Stanzas 23–24* (Present tense) showing the vision of past life dying back into the landscape. *Stanzas 25–26* (Past tense) the culmination of the tale itself: the "she-bird" and the man 'die' in sexual union, but phoenix-like rise to a new life.

l.29 THE QUICK OF NIGHT: a reversal of 'the dead of night'.

ll.42–43 Water turned into snowflakes is compared to manna, the 'bread' with which God fed the hungry Israelites; thus the "high corn" and the "harvest" melting on the birds' tongues are the falling snow itself.

[126]

ll.48–50 Like a "lost believer" or Satan ("the hurled outcast of light"), he seeks a divine rebirth ("inhuman cradle").

ll.54–55 He prays that the product of his union with the "engulfing bride" will not, like "seed" or "flesh", be subject to death.

l.121 FOR THE BIRD LAY BEDDED . . . : the sense runs on, not from the previous stanza, but from line 110, and explains how "the tale ended".

IN MY CRAFT OR SULLEN ART (October 1945)

Compare Yeats's *Sailing to Byzantium*.

A general comment in an essay by W. H. Auden seems a good approximation to the theme of this poem: "The impulse to create a work of art is felt when, in certain persons, the passive awe provoked by sacred beings or events is transformed into a desire to express that awe in a rite of worship or homage . . . nothing is expected in return."

Broken only in line 14, the basic pattern in each stanza is a series of 7-syllable lines ending in a final line of 6.

l.1 CRAFT OR SULLEN ART: Thomas viewed his poetry generally as a difficult *craft*. If it is an *art* at all, it is an art made "sullen" ('morose', 'gloomy') by that difficulty. But "sullen" here also means 'solitary', 'lonely'.

l.5 Embracing lovers hold all that concerns them in their arms.

l.6 SINGING LIGHT: the light of lamp or moon by which the poet 'sings'. (The lamp itself might be thought of as making a noise.)

ll.8–9 Cheap popularity (and financial reward) earned by flashy posturing.

IVORY also links with the word "*towering*" later (line 15) to suggest the 'ivory tower'—the usual image for art's sometimes unrealistic aloofness from ordinary human affairs.

ll.10–11 The poet's rewards are the same as those of the lovers—relationship, love, commitment to human limitations.

l.14 SPINDRIFT: light spray blown off the sea, suggesting here the impermanence of poetry.

l.15 TOWERING DEAD: either those in 'ivory towers', dead to the

world of ordinary life; or those dead men with "towering"
reputations already honoured by the "nightingales and
psalms" of life and literature.

FERN HILL (October 1945)

Compare Henry Vaughan's *The Retreate*, Wordsworth's *Ode:
Intimations of Immortality*, Philip Larkin's *I Remember, I Remember*
and Thomas's different treatment of the same farm in the first story
of his *Portrait of the Artist as a Young Dog*.

Fern Hill is a farm just outside Carmarthen. Thomas spent many
childhood holidays there at a time when it was the home of Ann
Jones, the aunt commemorated in *After the funeral*.

Only lines 6 and 52 break the syllabic count of 14, 14, 9, 6, 9, 14,
14 in the first seven lines of each stanza. And even the 7, 9, 7, 9, 9,
6; 9, 6, 9, 6, 7, 9 of the two final lines in each stanza would seem to
have a pattern. Equally consistent is the use of assonance (vowel
repetition) instead of rhymes at the line-endings (e.g. boughs-
towns, green-leaves, starry-barley, climb-eyes-light).

l.3 DINGLE: a small wooded valley.

l.4 HAIL AND CLIMB suggests stopping the hay-waggon and climbing
  aboard.

l.9 WINDFALL: prematurely fallen. A literal picture of light on early-
  fallen apples. "Windfall" also carries connotations of good
  luck.

ll. 13–14 A good example of how syntax allows several meanings at
  once: Time let him play and be golden; Time let him play
  and live ("be"); and Time let him play and left him alone
  ("let me . . . be").

l.20 TUNES FROM THE CHIMNEYS: smoke wafted on the air.

ll. 20–22 Notice the covert suggestion of the four elements—air,
  water, fire, earth.

  FIRE GREEN AS GRASS: fire as intense as grass is green.

ll.24–29 The childlike notion that, while the boy is asleep, the
  farm does not exist; that it exists in and for his own con-
  sciousness.

l.30 MAIDEN: by not mentioning Eve by name, the poet helps the idea that it was all his own (Adam's) world.

l.47 BY THE SHADOW OF MY HAND: hidden in the syntax is the common expression "take me . . . by the . . . hand". "Shadow", however, indicates the intangible touch of Time.

l.51 CHILDLESS LAND: "childless" because the child has grown up.

l.53 HELD: because of "chains" in the next line, "held" means 'chained'; but because of "mercy" in the previous line, it also suggests 'cradled', 'supported'.

ON A WEDDING ANNIVERSARY (February 1946)

The earliest printed version of this poem was longer and different in effect. But it confirms the fact that the setting is that of the wartime air-raids. With one exception, the syllabic count is 6, 10, 7, 7.

l.6 LOVE AND HIS PATIENTS: the horror of the bombing drives the man and wife mad. Love itself is seen as a demented asylum warder. Previously "in tune" (l.3), they now "roar on a chain".

ll.7–8 CRATER/CARRYING CLOUD: a cloud-like formation of falling bombs, which will cause the crater; or the cloud in which the aeroplane is flying.

l.9 THE WRONG RAIN: falling bombs.

l.10 "They come together" in the sense that they are finally made one in instantaneous death. In which case "parted" probably means 'made into separate individuals'. Formerly separate individuals, the violence of the bombs makes their bodies inseparable (notice the singular nouns which follow—"their *heart*", "their *brain*").

IN COUNTRY SLEEP (December 1947)

Compare Coleridge's *Frost at Midnight* and Yeats's *A Prayer for My Daughter*.

The poet addresses his sleeping daughter, urging her not to fear what children usually fear, the fantastic figures of fairy tales, nursery rhymes, and superstition. The countryside which is the source of these imagined characters is, itself, benign and safe. The only figure to fear is the Thief—Time, Experience, but mainly Death. And yet the very certainty of his coming shows he is part of the natural scheme of things. Safety from this real fear comes in an awareness of that planned pattern.

l.16 MY RIDER: his daughter, "riding" the world of dreams.

l.38 THE THIEF: image from the Bible, e.g. *2 Peter*, iii. 10: "But the day of the Lord will come as a thief in the night."

l.95 WOUND: in the poem "wound" seems to stand for 'heart'.

l.96 From this line onwards, the poet concentrates on words which suggest purpose and control: "designed", "truly", "ruly", "surely", "ship shape" etc.

l.104 The meaning would appear to demand a comma after "faith" in this line. Thus the sense of ll.99–106 is that the Thief comes to change her belief that he comes to steal her faith, and to change her belief that he comes to leave her forsaken.

OVER SIR JOHN'S HILL (May 1949)

Compare Hopkins's *The Windhover* and Ted Hughes's *The Hawk in the Rain*. Sir John's Hill overlooks the estuary in Laugharne.

l.2 THE HAWK ON FIRE HANGS STILL: "on fire" and "hangs" are the start of two main lines of imagery. Thus "on fire" (dynamic in action, and reflecting the sun) yields "rays", "fiery", "flash" (twice), "on fire", "fuse", "flames" etc.; and "hangs" yields images of guilt, execution, and judgment— "hoisted", "drop", "gallows", "tyburn", "noosed", "black cap", "just hill", "halter" etc. Thomas, as "young Aesop" (l.35), witnesses the hierarchy of natural death: the hawk kills the sparrows, but is itself "noosed".

ll. 21–2 cf. "Dilly dilly, come to be killed" in the nursery rhyme "Dilly Dilly".

l.33 WE: the poet and the heron.

l.51 TOWY: one of the rivers running into the estuary at Laugharne.

l.58 GRAVE: engrave.

[pages 84–8]

IN THE WHITE GIANT'S THIGH (September 1950)

Compare Thomas Hardy's *In Front of the Landscape*.

The poet walks over a "high chalk hill" (the White Giant of the title) at night, and imagines the former lives of the childless women lying buried there, and the survival of their longings even in death. There is, in fact, a white giant figure carved in chalk, associated with fertility superstition, at Cerne Abbas, Dorset.

A regular structure of fifteen rhymed quatrains is intentionally obscured by irregular layout.

l.1 RIVERS: presumably rivers of blood in the curlews' throats.

l.14 WAINS: waggons.

l.17 LIGHTED SHAPES OF FAITH: the stars.

l.29 HAWED: overgrown with wild thorn.

l.37 GAMBO: a common word in Wales for a haycart.

l.39 SHIPPEN: cowshed.

l.59 FOR EVER MERIDIAN: for ever at highest pitch or in their prime.

LAMENT (March 1951)

Compare Yeats's *The Wild Old Wicked Man*, and Louis MacNeice's *The Libertine*.

Of all the poems which Thomas included in his *Collected Poems* in 1952, this is the one which has the clearest affinities with the comic gusto of the poet's prose works and with some of the characterization in *Under Milk Wood*.

DO NOT GO GENTLE INTO THAT GOOD NIGHT (May 1951)

Compare Thomas's *Elegy* and William Empson's *To an Old Lady*. Addressed to the poet's father as he approached blindness and death. The relevant aspect of the relationship was Thomas's profound respect for his father's uncompromising independence of mind, now tamed by illness. In the face of strong emotion, the poet sets himself the task of mastering it in the difficult form of the villanelle. Five tercets are followed by a quatrain, with the first and last line of the first stanza repeated alternately as the last line of subsequent stanzas and gathered into a couplet at the end of the quatrain. And all this on only two rhymes. Thomas further compounds his difficulty by having each line contain 10 syllables.

The poem has strong echoes of Yeats's favourite words—"rage", "gay" and "blaze"—and the middle four stanzas, describing the common approach to death of four different types of men, recall the fifth section of Yeats's *Nineteen Hundred and Nineteen*.

l.5 HAD FORKED NO LIGHTNING: had given and brought no revelation.

l.8 IN A GREEN BAY: in a friendly world.

l.14 GAY: the same idea as Yeats's "tragic gaiety"—an exulting acceptance of life's tragedies, contrasted with the previous glum pessimism of the "grave men".

POEM ON HIS BIRTHDAY (Summer 1951)
Compare D. H. Lawrence's *The Ship of Death*.
The poem owes most of its imagery and atmosphere to its location in Laugharne. The "house on stilts" (l.4) is either the Boat House where the poet lived or the nearby shed where he did most of his writing at this time. He may have begun the poem as early as October 1949 if line 8—"His driftwood thirty-fifth wind turned age"—is intended literally.

With only one exception, the lines of each stanza alternate between 6 and 9 syllables. Assonance (agreement of vowels) replaces rhyme, and every stanza after the first has the same assonance-scheme.

l.23 WYNDS: a dialect word for 'alleys'.

l.38 ANGELUS: literally, a Catholic devotional exercise commemorating the Incarnation.

ll.42–45 The immediate future ("to-morrow") may have its cage torn open by "terror" (perhaps another war); but the ultimate future ("the dark") will be freed by love in death. What Thomas imagines from here on is not a Christian heaven, but a continuing process deprived of terror and uncertainty.

l.85 NIMBUS: bright cloud or halo.

[pages 92–4]

ELEGY ·

Compare *Do not go gentle into that good night*.

Left unfinished at the poet's death. The first seventeen lines are as Thomas left them. The present text was reconstructed from Thomas's manuscript by his friend Vernon Watkins, who explained that "Of the added lines sixteen are exactly as Dylan Thomas wrote them, and the remainder are only altered to the extent of an inversion or one or two words." It will be seen that a quatrain rhyme-scheme is counterpointed by the arrangement into stanzas of three lines. (Compare the arrangement of *In the white giant's thigh*.)

INDEX OF TITLES AND FIRST LINES

(*Small capitals indicate a title where that is completely different from a poem's first line.*)